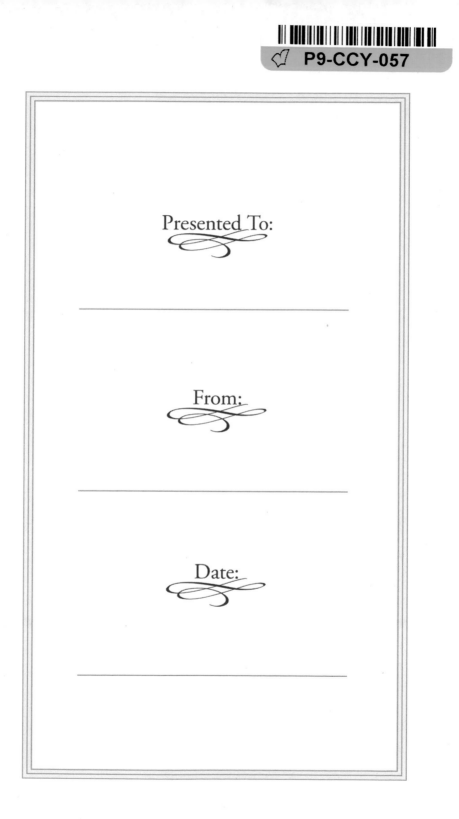

Presented To:

_____

From:

_____

Date:

_____

TURN THE WORLD UPSIDE DOWN

Discipling the Nations with
the Seven-Mountain Strategy

MICHAEL MAIDEN

DESTINY IMAGE® PUBLISHERS, INC.
P.O. Box 310, Shippensburg, PA 17257-0310
"Promoting Inspired Lives"

This book and all other Destiny Image, Revival Press, Mercy Place, Fresh Bread, Destiny Image Fiction, and Treasure House books are available at Christian bookstores and distributors worldwide.

For a U.S. bookstore nearest you, call 1-800-722-6774.
For more information on foreign distributors, call 717-532-3040.
Reach us on the Internet: www.destinyimage.com.

ISBN 13 TP: 978-0-7684-3885-7
ISBN 13 Ebook: 978-0-7684-8962-0

For Worldwide Distribution, Printed in the U.S.A.
1 2 3 4 5 6 7 8 9 10 11 / 13 12 11

Endorsements

The Kingdom lifestyle of the believer is capable of bringing about cultural transformation. But when the Church pulls back from the world, not wanting to be contaminated by its darkness, we lose our voice and influence. Can we influence society without becoming like it? Yes. In fact, we must! Dr. Michael Maiden's *Turn the World Upside Down* helps by identifying the seven major mountains of influence established in society. By targeting these realms, it becomes possible for each one of us to maximize our place of influence where we are most gifted. Dr. Maiden addresses this topic with great wisdom and practical insight. Books like *Turn the World Upside Down* help me to realize that our dream of presenting entire cities and nations to Jesus is actually doable.

Bill Johnson
Pastor of Bethel Church, Redding, California
Author, *When Heaven Invades Earth* and *Face to Face With God*

The Church was always called to possess and occupy—to dynamically and aggressively fill the earth with the knowledge of the glory of the Lord. As believers, we are to influence and change the world around us; we were never called to have the world change us. In his book *Turn the World Upside Down* Dr. Michael Maiden has skillfully, under the anointing of the Holy

Spirit, laid out an apostolic strategy that is attainable for all. *Turn the World Upside Down* built my faith, clarified my focus, and ignited fresh fire in my heart for the Church's commission to "Go ye therefore…." This book should be in every believer's library. It is a now word and a must-read. Yes, a must-read!

Patricia King
Founder of XPmedia
XPmedia.com

In a world appearing to be and feeling as if it is spinning out of control, in a season of time when the Church is having little success in affecting society, and in a time of paradigm shifting, there is a longing, if not a crying, for more than encouragement in our distress: We need direction and answers.

Dr. Michael Maiden delivers both. He exposes seven areas of unconquered territory and shows the way to possess what God has given us. His challenge, if accepted, will indeed *Turn the World Upside Down*.

I recommend that you read this book several times before passing it on.

Iverna Tompkins, DD, DLitt

My dear friend Pastor Mike Maiden has consistently been on the cutting edge of what the Lord is doing in the earth. His keen prophetic gift has served to make a significant impact on the lives of multiplied believers both in Phoenix, Arizona, and all around the world. As we begin to move forward toward what many are calling a new apostolic reformation, it is essential that we begin to realize that we have a cultural mandate inherent in the Gospel of the Kingdom. We are called to influence and disciple nations. Our paradigm and our worldview as the people of God is being enlarged to align with Christ's intention for the nations. As Pastor Mike unfolds the necessity for a greater understanding of the Gospel of the Kingdom, my prayer is that you will discover, in a fresh way, your responsibility and part that God has called you to play in the restoration He is bringing to the earth in this hour. Thanks, Pastor Mike, for lifting your voice like a trumpet and once again prophetically speaking to this generation!

Dr. Mark Chironna
The Master's Touch International Church
Mark Chironna Ministries
Orlando, Florida

Turn the World Upside Down is truly one of the best books I've read on the relevant, significant topic of the seven mountains. Dr. Maiden's engaging discussion on the call of today's Church to regain its influence over these prominent focal areas of our society and our culture make this a must-read for Christians everywhere: pastors, leaders, and church members alike. His insights demonstrate spiritual inspiration as well as qualified expertise of the subject matter, and Mike's writing style propels one effortlessly through the book. I literally couldn't put it down! I highly recommend *Turn the World Upside Down*. I know I'll read it again and again.

Dr. Lawrence Kennedy
President and Senior Pastor, North Church
President and Bishop, Church on the Rock International

Acknowledgements:

My dear friend, Dr. Lance Wallnau, whose genius captured the wisdom of God expressed through Bill Bright, Lauren Cunningham, and Francis Schaeffer.

Larry Witton, what an awesome blessing you are!

My beloved parents, Richard and Carol Maiden, who taught me the Kingdom of God.

The beautiful people of Church for the Nations.

Contents

Foreword by Lance Wallnau

I have been waiting for this book for a long time and am delighted that Dr. Michael Maiden was the one who wrote it. Mike has been an inspiration to me for over 15 years. He and Kim Clement prophetically fueled the quest in my life that led me to a life-changing interview in Kelowna, British Columbia, and my first vision of the seven mountains.

The year was 2000, and I was speaking at a conference in Canada along with Loren Cunningham. He told me about the historic moment when he, as head of *Youth With A Mission*, first met Bill Bright of *Campus Crusade*. These two leaders of the two largest youth organizations met as a sort of merging of streams, one strongly evangelical and the other shaped by Pentecostal and Charismatic influences. They found their common ground instantly as both produced diagrams they had received while meditating on the Great Commission. They each described the same seven spheres of influence that needed to be penetrated by the next generation. Loren called them "mind molders" and Bill described them as "world kingdoms." This meeting of generals happened in 1974, but I was only hearing about it in 2000. Why? It seemed to me that the significance of that historic moment and its insight was largely lost. Since 2000 I have made it my quest to get this message out. That's why this book *Turn The World Upside Down* excites me.

The first stage of any powerful idea begins with theorists who generate ideas, moves to researchers who revise and validate ideas, moves on to teachers who popularize ideas, and finally reaches practitioners who translate those ideas into tangible models. During the last decade I've seen a vast company embrace the seven-mountain template, but what has been needed are runners who can take this to the next level—and that is where Dr. Michael Maiden enters the arena. Here is a man who not only brings added illumination and excitement to the message, he challenges the status quo by furnishing a practical model of how to make this message work in a local community. How so? Dr. Mike actively pastors one of North America's fastest-growing churches, with five campuses and 6,000 people—and growing—while preaching this message.

As I read the manuscript, I was arrested by Mike's fresh grasp of the subject. At the very first chapter entitled "It Isn't Working!" he states, "Before ascending to Heaven, Jesus commissioned the apostles to *'Go therefore and make disciples of all the nations....'* ...After two millennia, the Church has made disciples *in* nations but not *of* nations." That sentence hit me like a stun gun—I've never heard it put that way before. Then he follows this thrust with a powerful question: "Could we have traded jobs with Jesus and expected Him to disciple nations while we build churches? ...We have mistakenly made the Gospel we preach exclusively about adding people to the church and have ignored discipling our cities, states, and nations." Clearly this is a new breed of pastor.

Mike's perspective is multifaceted because he is a man who has journeyed up more than one mountain. His professional training is not only in theology; he has climbed to the summit of the education mountain as well with an earned master's and doctorate degree in psychology. Doing so has given him a profound appreciation for the application of the Gospel to the brokenness of the human condition. He has a unique perspective on how the call of God answers the deep longing for fulfillment in the human heart. Like few others, Mike has the ability to forge a bridge between the individual, the Kingdom, churches, and the seven mountains.

Mike connects the individual and the seven mountains by early on addressing the one question people ask most frequently, "What is my mountain?" Mike's answer is brilliant: "The mountain of influence to which you are called is the place where you will find the job you love, financial success, people you enjoy being with, and ultimate personal fulfillment. Your position in your mountain, the one that God has prepared for you and the one for which you have been prepared, is your 'sweet spot,' your perfect fit. Not only is it God's place where you can most effectively bring to bear His presence and power to affect an area of your culture, but it is also *your place.* If you were a key, the position God called you to would be a lock in which you fit perfectly—the lock on the door of your destiny." This is the Great Commission put into language that will for the first time capture the imagination of everyone who is disengaged—especially youth. Find your mountain and you will be 100 percent alive! No doubt, this is part of what makes Pastor Mike's people and church campuses grow.

Each chapter pulsates with fresh insight on this momentous subject. This is a must-read for every present or potential pastor, politician, educator, entertainer, engineer, lawyer, business owner, salesperson, intercessor, and artist. This is a book that inspires exploits and will stir the disengaged and make them want to be engaged.

I have been waiting for this book because I have believed for some time that God will start to raise heralds in each mountain who will articulate and embody the pathway to success. Dr. Maiden is standing atop the church mountain, and with this book he breathes into us the vision to take all seven!

Lance Wallnau
Lancelearning@mac.com
www.lancelearning.com

CHAPTER ONE
It Isn't Working!

Before ascending to Heaven, Jesus commissioned the apostles to *"Go therefore and make disciples of all the nations..."* (Matt. 28:19). After two millennia, the Church has made disciples *in* nations but not *of* nations. We need to consider whether our understanding of the Gospel and way of doing church is flawed. Is something wrong? And if it is, how can we fix it?

Over the past 2,000 years, there have been powerful moves of God on the earth, yet few of them have had a lasting effect upon nations. In the history of our own country, we have experienced outpourings like the divine healing movements, the outpouring of the baptism of the Holy Spirit at Azusa Street and other locations, the Charismatic Renewal, and powerful moves of God in various places.

These outpourings brought people to Christ, changed lives, and revived God's people but had little effect upon our nation.

Not only has there been no improvement in our culture, but we have also seen our nation and the world become progressively *more* ungodly. We are actually losing ground! Perhaps it is time for another approach.

> In Acts 17:6, the Bible tells us that Paul and Silas were said to have *"... turned the world upside down."* So we have to wonder why today's church is not "turning our world upside down."

The Gospel we preach is not wrong or bad, but could it be incomplete? If we are not discipling nations, then something must be missing from our understanding of our *purpose,* our *mission,* our *doctrine,* our *teaching,* and our practice of "doing church." Yes, we have seen souls saved and lives changed (and that is *very* important), but we have failed to transform our cities and the nations. Where have we missed it?

Doctrine of Defeat?

With courage and an open mind, we should reconsider our understanding of God's ultimate purpose for the Church, considering the possibility that we have seen our mission through church-eyes and not Kingdom-eyes.

Second Chronicles 12:9-10 tells about a happening during the reign of Solomon's son Rehoboam:

> *Shishak king of Egypt came up against Jerusalem, and took the treasures of the house of the LORD and the treasures of the king's palace. He took everything; he even took the golden shields which Solomon had made. Then King Rehoboam made shields of bronze in their place...* (NASB).

This seemingly minor incident in the history of Israel provides us a major insight: The removal of the treasures from the house of the Lord, particularly the gold, symbolizes the removal of divine truth and glory from the Church. Although Rehoboam continued the religious practices of Solomon, something important was missing. The Church had a similar experience during the Middle Ages.

For about 1,000 years, from about A.D. 500 to 1500, there was a spiritual, intellectual, and invasive darkness upon the earth. During that time known as the Dark Ages, a cloud of despair settled over the world because the revelatory light of God was dimmed. (God always has a remnant, but they were few and their voice was weak.) During this period, the understanding of God's Word, like Solomon's treasure, was stolen from His people. The Church replaced revelatory truth with legalism, tradition, and even idolatry.

Instead of acknowledging before God that something was missing and asking Him for its return, Rehoboam lived in denial and substituted shields made from a common metal for those that had been made of precious gold. Likewise, the present-day church is in denial about its failure to affect culture and has substituted doctrines of defeat to justify its failure to carry out God's intention to "disciple nations."

During Solomon's reign, the gold shields glistened in the sun, proclaiming God's blessing, presence, and power. The bronze shields, although they may have been the same size and shape, were merely pale imitations of the "real thing." No matter how much effort was put into polishing these counterfeits, they could never sparkle like those made from gold. Thus, the Church of the Dark Ages developed shiny imitations of spirituality that were pale substitutes for the power, presence, and purpose of God.

The Church of that day tried to replace what it had lost with impressive cathedrals, stained-glass windows, lavish ceremonies, ostentatious garments, and the like. Most of the "religious" things that came into the Church of that day did not come out of evil intent but resulted from good people trying to "assist" God. The Church of today is little better. We have tried to help God by replacing *His ways* with *our programs* and by imitating His purpose to change the world with a doctrine that merely justifies our seeming powerlessness to influence it. When you replace the golden treasures of the Kingdom with the cheap imitation of traditions, Jesus warned:

> *You are nullifying and making void and of no effect [the authority of] the Word of God through your tradition, which you [in turn] hand on. And many things of this kind you are doing* (Mark 7:13 AMP).

When Truth Was Lost From the Church

Instead of pleading with God for the restoration of His glory, the Church substituted something else for it. Like Adam and Eve who covered themselves with clothing of their own making instead of coming to God naked, admitting their *neediness,* and asking for help, the Church too has tried to cover its spiritual emptiness with things of human design. Many in the Church have settled for a substitute of God's presence, purpose, and power, and the Church's attempt to clothe itself is like the emperor's new wardrobe. The world sees the nakedness of the Church and says, "That isn't good enough for us. Show us the real thing or get out of our face!"

Some in today's Church are like to Apollos in the story found in Acts 18:24-26:

Now a certain Jew named Apollos, born at Alexandria, an eloquent man and mighty in the Scriptures, came to Ephesus. This man had been instructed in the way of the Lord; and being fervent in spirit, he spoke and taught accurately the things of the Lord, though he knew only the baptism of John. …When Aquila and Priscilla heard him, they took him aside and explained to him the way of God more accurately.

What Apollos knew, he knew well and preached boldly and passionately, but he only understood the "baptism of John" for repentance from sin. Two local Christians, Aquila and Priscilla, took him aside and explained the fullness of the Good News, and he became a powerful voice for the Gospel. Like Apollos, some have done what they know to do (getting souls saved) and in some cases did it well, but now it is time for Christians to awaken to the Church's *ultimate* purpose, to relearn a fuller and richer truth about bringing a lost world to Christ.

Restoration Reformation

Not quite 500 years ago, God began restoring truth to His Church, beginning with Martin Luther and the restoration of the foundational truth of salvation through grace (not works). Martin Luther shook the world when he nailed his "95 Theses" to the door of the Wittenberg chapel. He declared that instead of buying or earning forgiveness and purchasing one's way to Heaven, salvation is a gift that cannot be purchased and only comes through God's grace. Today, we take this most basic of truths for granted, but it was lost to humanity for almost ten centuries.

Since that time, there has been a progressive and gradual restoration of truth. Each reestablished truth was considered by many at that time to be newfound doctrine, but these truths have proven to be the reinstatement of something vital that had been lost. Following Luther's breakthrough came:

- The restoration of water baptism

- The outpouring of divine healing

- The recognition of the baptism of the Holy Spirit

It took almost 400 years for these fundamental truths to be restored, but today the restoration of truth is moving more quickly. Recently, the understanding that faith can move God has been relearned, and there has been a reestablishing of the fivefold ministry: apostles, prophets, teacher, pastors, and evangelists (see Eph. 4:11-13). With the return of each new truth and the knowledge of God's original intent, the Church has increased and so has its power.

Are We Preaching the Gospel Jesus Preached?

For centuries, the Church has focused on preaching and teaching the Gospel of Christ, or salvation, which is repentance, forgiveness, and going to Heaven. But is that the Gospel Jesus preached? Instead of imitating

Christ's ministry, we have "improved" on it. We do not teach what He taught; we teach who He was and what He did. *It is not wrong or evil to teach the Gospel of Christ.* However, the Gospel of Christ is *not* the Gospel Jesus preached or the Gospel He commissioned His disciples to preach. It also is not the Gospel of the early Church. We cannot have the results that Jesus, the apostles, and early Church had and promote a different Gospel.

The first words Jesus preached were, *"The kingdom of God is near. Repent and believe the good news!"* (see Mark 1:15 NIV). Jesus *was not saying*, as the Church has taught, "Repent, go to church, live a good life, and when you die you will go to Heaven." Jesus *was saying* that repentance opens the door for Heaven to come to earth. The world hungers for the real thing, and it is waiting for us to declare the *real* Gospel of Christ—the Gospel of the Kingdom.

The word *kingdom* is used more than 40 times in the New Testament, but the word *church* is used only twice in the Gospels. One of those times found in Matthew 16:18, where Jesus said, *"I will build My church..."* (KJV). Later He commanded His disciples in Matthew 28:19 that *they* were to *"make disciples of all nations"* (NIV). Could we have traded jobs with Jesus and expected Him to disciple nations while we build churches? The Church has an important function in God's Kingdom, but we have mistakenly made the Gospel we preach exclusively about adding people to the Church and have ignored discipling our cities, states, and nations.

Surrender of the Church

For the most part, the born-again Church has decided it cannot change Hollywood or the culture of America, and it has taken another path. Because of our seeming impotence at influencing our culture, we have tried to vindicate ourselves with a doctrine that says we will try to save as many people as possible, take them to Heaven with us, and leave the rest to go to hell.

Cultural Hermits

Many Christians live a cloistered life promoted by their churches. Similar to the monks of the Middle Ages, we have huddled together in our own little subculture made up exclusively of Christian friends, Christian novels, Christian music, and Christian television. Although none of those things are wrong or bad in themselves, they have removed us from the very thing we have been called to change: our society. We have believed that God expects us to avoid exposing ourselves to the wickedness of the world when all along He wanted to use us to expose His goodness to the world.

Jesus *is* coming soon! However, He will not come until the Church finishes its job of discipling nations and begins the process of making the kingdoms of this world into *"the kingdom of our Lord and of His Christ…"* (Rev. 11:15 NIV). However, we have mostly preached a defeated Christianity, and by our actions and inactions, we have declared that we:

- Don't worry about politics, business, entertainment, or the rest of society.

- Don't worry about corruption, disease, poverty, or any other ills of society.

With billions of souls on the road to damnation, the Church has lavishly prayed for the rapture, "Oh, God," we've cried out, "Come! Come and take us away because everything is becoming so evil." Yet, how could things get better when the Church has, in most cases, withdrawn its influence from our culture and even cursed society by declaring that things are "just getting worse and worse"? The bestselling Christian books of recent times, such as *The Late Great Planet Earth* and *Left Behind*, are not about living victoriously for Christ and taking back what the devil has stolen but about escaping before the devil completely takes over. We have believed a theology that says the enemy will overwhelm the Church and Christians will barely escape at the last moment. And yet, is it not curious that the Bible speaks of the last days as the "Day of the Lord" rather than the "day of the devil"?

A Gospel of Fear

Feeling incapable of attracting the masses with a powerless message, the Church has preached a Gospel intended to scare the hell out of sinners. The Church throughout the ages has tried to use fear to motivate people into the Kingdom, while all the time the Bible says, *"...God's kindness is intended to lead you to repent (to change your mind and inner man to accept God's will)"* (Rom. 2:4 AMP).

God's #1 Priority for Planet Earth

When Jesus was instructing His disciples (and us) in Matthew 6:9-13 how to pray, He first said to pray, *"Thy Kingdom come."* It is no accident that Jesus mentions this first. It was not merely an elegant way to structure a prayer that He knew countless people would repeat. By placing the Kingdom first in His model prayer, Jesus was saying that establishing the Kingdom of God on earth is *God's number one priority*. Yet, the Church failed to understand and surmised that this was merely a euphemism for salvation. Salvation is vitally important because it is the only way into God's Kingdom, but "the Kingdom" is more than salvation; the Gospel of the Kingdom is the fullness of God's intention for our world.

"Your will be done on earth" is the next phrase in the Lord's Prayer. Yet, the Church has shown more concern for Heaven than earth. God obviously wants the earth to return to His will and His way of doing things. However, the Church has mostly refused to participate in God's plan. Our emphasis has been on Heaven rather than bringing His will to our planet. Many have believed, "The earth doesn't matter. God's just going to burn it up anyway." Because of our lack of understanding about salvation and our misplaced emphasis on the rapture and the tribulation, the Church has mostly failed to fulfill its purpose in society, and satan has stepped into the vacuum created by our absence.

Jesus' preaching about the coming Kingdom of God was not the first time the concept of God's governance of earth is mentioned in Scripture. In fact, it was God's plan from the beginning, and He has no Plan B. Genesis 1:27-28 says:

> *So God created man in His own image; in the image of God He created him; male and female He created them. Then God blessed them, and God said to them, "Be fruitful and multiply;* ***fill the earth and subdue it*** *[conquer any adversity to My Kingdom];* ***have dominion*** *over the fish of the sea, over the birds of the air, and over every living thing that moves on the earth."*

God was saying, "I created earth, it is Mine, but I am making humankind the steward over the earth." Man was to be His viceroy, His earthly governor and ambassador. God then stepped aside and empowered people to govern the earth. God could do that with confidence because He had created humankind in His image. However, when man sinned and lost the image of God, he lost dominion, authority, and the capacity to rule the earth wisely, and that dominion and authority was transferred to another.

Authority to Reign

During the temptation of Jesus in the wilderness following His water baptism, satan offered Jesus all the kingdoms of the world. Bear in mind that a thing can only be a temptation if it is something the other person wants and you have the ability to grant it. Luke 4:5-6 says:

> The devil led Him up to a high place and showed Him in an instant all the kingdoms of the world. And he said to Him, "I will give You all their authority and splendor, for it has been given ['betrayed' in the Greek] to me, and I can give it to anyone I want to" (NIV).

From this Scripture, we learn some important things:

- Satan took Jesus to a high mountain (mountains in Scripture often stand for authority).

- The kingdoms of earth belonged to satan, and he had the power to confer his authority over them to a person of his choice (the devil governed the earth).

- The kingdoms of earth were given to him (Adam gave away his authority and right to rule when he sinned and lost the image of God).

- Jesus wanted to take back authority over the kingdoms (nations) of the earth.

Jesus refused satan's offer even though it represented a painless way to achieve His ultimate purpose of reconciling the world to God. Jesus' mission was to redeem humankind (to restore man to the image of God and the Adamic covenant) and to return authority over the earth and the devil to humanity. Psalm 115:16, explains, "The heavens belong to the Lord, but He has given the earth to all humanity" (NLT). God's purpose for humankind has never changed. Redeemed man still has the marching orders given to Adam: Subdue the earth and take dominion over it. We are not called to "hold the fort" until Jesus comes but to sally forth and take back what the enemy has stolen (the kingdoms of earth).

Have You Ever Wondered...

...or perhaps been asked why a loving God allows horrendous things on the earth—poverty, sickness, war, sexual slavery, injustice, and other forms of suffering? The answer is: God does nothing on earth except by permission since giving the earth to humankind. The governance of fallen, ungodly men and women and the acceptance of satan's defiling presence have brought about all the suffering and evil on the earth. Christ's purpose was to take back what Adam gave to satan and restore the mandate of the Garden of Eden so that the world could once again come under the control of redeemed men and women operating in the will of God.

Romans 5:17 explains the restoration of dominion like this:

*For if, by the trespass of the one man, **death reigned** through that one man, how much more will those who receive God's abundant provision of grace and of the gift of righteousness **reign in life** through the one man, Jesus Christ* (NIV).

Righteousness restores rulership and causes the redeemed to "reign in life." Notice that we are not reigning in Heaven but *on* earth *in* this life. When we are thinking right, believing right, and speaking right, we have the authority to reign through Christ.

However, the Kingdom of God will not come to the earth through violence, political activities, or humanitarian efforts. In fact, according to Jesus in John 3:3, you cannot even "see the Kingdom" unless you are born again. And, He went on to declare that those who are *not* born again *"cannot enter the Kingdom of God"* (John 3:5).

The born-again Church has piled up people at the entryway of the Kingdom. They have come through the gates by the blood of Christ and entered the lobby of salvation. Yet, according to John 14:2, *There are many rooms in My Father's house.... I am going there to prepare a place for you*" (NCV). Each room is filled with spiritual treasure waiting to be possessed. Unfortunately, most Christians are standing in the lobby waiting for the King to come while the King is waiting for them to claim their spiritual treasures and fulfill the purpose of their redemption. He is waiting for us to put on Christ and become the glorious last-day Church that is "without spot or wrinkle" (see Eph. 5:27).

"Give Me My Mountain!"

The Church has traditionally defined *revival* as a restoration of passion for God and personal sanctification, and that is good, important, and has its place. However, the Church has never accepted that revival should grow and mature to the point where it achieved God's ultimate purpose—to transform neighborhoods, cities, and states and to "disciple nations."

Just as "mountains" in the Bible usually represent the authority of kingdoms, "hills" represent elements of government. Bear that in mind while reading what the prophet Isaiah said when speaking of the last days (our day):

> *Now it shall come to pass in the latter days that **the mountain of the LORD's house shall be established on the top of the mountains**, and shall be exalted above the hills; **and all nations shall flow to it**. Many people shall come and say, "Come, and let us go up to the mountain of the LORD..."* (Isaiah 2:2-3).

The elements of culture that make up every nation can be described as *seven mountains*. When the Church loses its influence in the seven mountains of society, it fails to advance the Kingdom of God. God's plan since the beginning of time was for the righteous to impact culture, not for culture to impact the Church. *Every born-again person is called to a place of influence in at least one of the seven mountains of culture*:

- *Family*—The first mountain. By the design of God, the family is the place where righteousness is to be taught, personal character developed, and Kingdom destiny discovered.

- *Church*—The Church was birthed by Jesus Christ and is ordained and anointed to equip humankind to experience and expand the Kingdom of God on earth.

- *Business*—The purpose for believers in business is to advance the Kingdom of God through displaying Christlikeness, deploying godly influence, and the faithful and righteous stewardship of wealth.

- *Government*—The concept and creation of human government is from God. The success or failure of any form or level of government depends upon the personal character, wisdom, and justice of those in leadership.

- *Education*—Education is vitally important, and the primary instruments of education are the family and the church. The means, method, and mission of the educators determine the result.

- *Arts/Entertainment*—The arts belong to God. Creativity and giftedness come from God. We are on the verge of a modern-day renaissance birthed out of a new apostolic reformation in the Church.

- *Media*—Communication is power. The mountain of media is the voice of a culture. To change a culture, the influence of media must be transformed.

Darkness has descended upon the mountains of culture. That darkness is a demonic dominion that brings suffering to humanity through that mountain's influence upon society. God has called His people to climb to positions of influence in these seven mountains and restore the Kingdom of God to our society.

The Kingdom of God *Will* Be Established!

When believers discover their personal callings and invade their individual mountains, they will have uncommon favor, supernatural wisdom and understanding, and divine empowerment to transform those mountains.

God informs us in Isaiah 2:2 that in the last days, *"...The* LORD's *house shall be established* **on the top of the mountains...."** His Kingdom will rule over all the kingdoms of this earth when a generation of believers understands its purpose and mission and takes its place in the seven mountains and through those mountains influences the culture of the nations.

The *real* purpose of the Church is to equip and train people to take their mountains for God. It is the season for the Church to do its job and for Christians to catch God's vision for the last day and receive an impartation of zeal to "be about the Father's business." When they do, they will cry out to God as Caleb did to Joshua upon entering the Promised Land—"Give me my mountain!"—and He will.

CHAPTER TWO
Back to the Future

Have you ever wondered why, after completing His work of modeling the life of a believer, dying on the Cross to reconcile the world to God, descending to hell and taking the keys of authority from satan, and rising from the dead, Jesus didn't establish His Kingdom on earth right then and there? We learned in the last chapter that God's purpose is to establish His Kingdom and for His will to be done on earth. So, after doing all the hard work, why did Jesus leave for Heaven?

> *But when this priest* [Christ] *had offered for all time one sacrifice for sins, He sat down at the right hand of God. Since that time **He waits for His enemies to be made His footstool*** (Hebrews 10:12-13 NIV).

Why Are We Here?

When Saul, the persecutor of Christians, fell to the ground under the spotlight of God and had his dramatic encounter with Christ on the road to Damascus (see Acts 9), he asked the necessary question, the one each of us must also ask: "Lord, what do You want me to do?"

What does God expect of believers? What is the Church's purpose? The obvious answer is found in the Great Commission:

Matthew 28:18-19 Unpacked

Then Jesus came to them and said, "All authority in heaven and on earth has been given to Me. Therefore go and make disciples of all nations, baptizing them in the name of the Father and of the Son and of the Holy Spirit, and teaching them to obey everything I have commanded you..." (Matthew 28:18-20 NIV).

- *"Authority"*—Much of the Church misses the clear implication that the Body of Christ has Jesus' authority *on the earth.* Therefore, the most powerful force on earth is not satan, the antichrist, Islam, socialism, communism, or any other "isms."

- *"All authority"*—This means that the Lord Jesus Christ, His Word, His Spirit, and His Church are *the* most powerful force on the earth.

- *"Go and make disciples of all the nations"*—In light of the revelation of the power now available to believers, Jesus released His disciples to go and take the Good News that God's Kingdom has come to the nations.

The similar passage in Mark 16:15 begins, *"Go into all the world...."* In spite of the command to go, the Church has mostly encouraged Christians to retreat from the world, to leave all the realms of influence in which they are called to be "salt and light." We have understood this passage to mean that we should send missionaries to convert the people of the far corners of the earth, and that is an important part of the Great Commission. However, we failed for the most part to teach our new converts to convert their cultures by bringing God's Kingdom into the seven mountains of their societies.

God's End-Time Emphasis

In the middle of His famous teaching about the end times, Jesus placed an often-overlooked, frequently misinterpreted, but revealing verse: Matthew 24:14.

Matthew 24:14 Unpacked

And this gospel of the kingdom will be preached in the whole world as a testimony to all nations, and then the end will come (Matthew 24:14 NIV).

This Scripture teaches:

- *"This Gospel of the Kingdom"*—The full Gospel, which includes the Gospel of salvation, is to be preached as a demonstration of God's love and ownership of the earth.

- *"Nations"*—We are to take this Gospel to nations that are made up of not only people but also the elements of their culture.

- *"Then the end will come"*—This means Jesus is delayed from returning until the elements that make up the cultures of the nations have been exposed to the Gospel of the Kingdom.

The Gospel of Christ—Christ the Savior, Healer, Baptizer, and soon-coming King—is the pillar of our faith. The Church emerged from 1,000 years of the Dark Ages having relearned the vital truth of salvation by faith and has preached salvation ever since. As important as salvation is, it is not the fullness of the Gospel that Jesus preached.

In our day, God is challenging the Church to preach and walk in the truths of the *full* Gospel, the Gospel of the early Church—the Gospel of the Kingdom of God. The salvation message has the power to change lives, but the Gospel of the Kingdom has the ability to transforms nations, cultures, and generations.

Jesus taught, "Repent, the Kingdom of God is at hand" (see Mark 1:15). According to Jesus, repenting, or finding salvation, as we would say, was not the end but the first step and only way into the Kingdom of God. We are called to get people born again, but we are also called to "disciple" or train them to reach their world, cities, and nations by bringing Christ into the seven mountains of culture:

- Family

- Education

- Religion

- Government

- Business

- Media

- Arts and Entertainment

Straightening up a Bent-Over World

The seven mountains represent every aspect of a nation's culture and all the realms of a person's life experience. Whoever controls a mountain controls that mountain's influence on a nation's culture. For example, when the Church leaves the media mountain, we lose the voice and influence we could bring to transform people who are within the influence that mountain provides. Our immoral, dysfunctional culture reflects the loss of influence in all seven mountains.

Myles Munroe defined the word *kingdom* like this:

A kingdom is the governing influence of a king over his territory, impacting it with his personal will, purpose, and intent, producing a culture, values, morals, and lifestyle that reflect the king's desires and nature for his citizens.[1]

God owns the earth, and He wants us to understand our role of returning it to the godly state He intended. This is what Romans 8:19 is talking about when it says, *"For the earnest expectation of the creation eagerly waits for the revealing of the sons of God."* God and all creation are waiting for a people who will enter into the fullness of what it means to be a "son of God," a people who will partner with Him to bring His culture back to all the earth.

Luke 13:11 tells of a woman who was "bent over" with sickness who "could not straighten up herself." She could not help herself, and no one could help her, but when Jesus saw her, He felt compassion and declared that she was "loosed." He touched her, and she straightened up. In the same way, we are called to minister to those in our society who are bent over with heaviness, heartache, demonic powers, sickness and disease, drug addiction, sadness, perversion, and every other bondage of satan. We have been empowered to say to those who are bent over by anything and everything, "I serve a God who will straighten you up. In the name of Jesus, be healed!"

Martin Luther said, "A gospel that does not deal with the issues of the day is not the Gospel at all." A Church that does not have Good News for the issues of the day is pushed out of the conversation when people try to solve problems. We have to regain our seat at the table of the brokers of power, and it is beginning to happen.

Prayer Solves Two Serial Murder Investigations

The police of Phoenix could not solve a series of murders that caused fear and panic to spread throughout the metropolitan area. One man had killed 12 people and another had killed 8 people, and no one knew when or where they might strike again. This continued for 18 months without law enforcement finding the perpetrators. So in desperation, having done all they could without results, the mayor of Phoenix sent letters to the churches requesting them to "please pray." Every church across the valley began praying from their pulpits, and within less than two weeks, the people responsible had been apprehended. This demonstrated to the mayor and to the church a role that it can play within the community.

Why the Church Lost Its Influence in the Seven Mountains

First, we have been separated from God. The enemy did not have to defeat us; we simply disobeyed God, which entitled satan to take positions of influence that rightfully belong to us. There is no such thing as a spiritual vacuum; when Christians yield their places of authority and influence, the enemy rushes in to fill the void. The spiritual law is: Any ground you don't take, you lose.

The Church has mistakenly measured its success by the wrong things—size of a congregation, money in the offering plate, buildings, even the presence of the glory of God in services. These are all good things, but they are not the right measuring stick. The measure of the Church's accomplishment is its success in transforming communities and nations. God measures the success of a pastor's ministry not by the size of his church but by whether lives are being changed and transformed. God uses the same measure for each Christian. He is looking to see if we are changing and transforming our world from the places of influence He has purposed for us to take.

We've Missed It, but We Have Another Chance

If My people who are called by My name will humble themselves, and pray and seek My face, and turn from their wicked ways, then I will hear from heaven, and will forgive their sin and heal their land (2 Chronicles 7:14).

It is never too late for God to heal the land!

There is a battle raging in the Church concerning eschatology (study of last things). The majority of evangelical Christians in America believe that the earth and the nations are so polluted, corrupted by evil, and devastated by sin that change for the good is hopeless. They have decided that it is a waste of effort to try to convert the government, bring Christ to business, or try to influence education. So they are trying to save souls and hang on until Christ comes again to straighten things out.

However, there are others who believe that we are here to change things. In fact, we believe that the early Church did just that: Less than 100 years after the establishment of the Church, the Roman Empire began to topple. It was not hordes of barbarians who brought down the greatest empire in the world. They merely took advantage of a weakened realm. It was the faith of believers that ended that godless empire. Also, communism in the Soviet Union was brought down through the prayers of the underground church. (Can China be far behind?)

We are also not engaged in the culture. We have told our children they could not be actors, musicians, or politicians or enter any other professions that would put them in places of influence because those places are "evil." The world is evil, but it is not our enemy; it is our assignment, our target. We easily forget that people are not our enemy.

Our struggle is not against flesh and blood, but against the rulers, against the authorities, against the powers of this dark world and against the spiritual forces of evil in the heavenly realms (Ephesians 6:12 NIV).

The local church has operated more like a cruise liner than a battleship. It is like a floating buffet with all-you-can-eat or -drink Christianity. On a battleship, you will find people who are always on the alert, focused, and ready to attack or repel the enemy, whereas on a cruise liner, the people are focused entirely on themselves and their own pleasures. If you were to sound an alarm and warn over the loudspeakers those on the cruise liner that they were under attack by pirates, most of the people onboard would not even stir from their deck chairs. They would merely say, "What? That can't be right. This is the love boat."

It is not enough to have Christians at the top of the seven mountains; Christians in places of influence must have a culture-changing faith. As I mentioned before, people can no longer be scared into Heaven, and they do not even want to know how to get to Heaven. They want to know how to:

- Pay their bills

- Have a good marriage

- Have kids who don't go crazy

- Be healthy in soul, mind, and body

- Find personal significance and meaning

- Find out why they are here.

However, the Church has told them, "Get saved, and get your ticket to Heaven. We can't do much for you here but everything will be great over there."

Consider this: If getting saved was our sole purpose in life, then as soon as we were born again, the smartest thing for God to do would be to kill us before we blew it and backslid.

Psalm 110:1 Unpacked

The LORD [the Father] *said to my Lord* [the Son], *"Sit at My right hand, till I make Your enemies Your footstool."*

Dispensationalists consign this statement to the Millennium, the 1,000-year reign of Christ on the earth described in Revelation 20:2-7. However, David was given a prophetic peek into Heaven at the moment Christ returned after completing His work on earth. The Father was saying to the Son that each of His victories would make it possible for His followers to build for Him a footstool. His work was done, and now He could sit and watch the Church (the Body of Christ) conquer the kingdoms of the earth.

We Stand at the Banks of the Jordan

The Church today stands (symbolically) where the children of Israel stood when they were on the edge of the Promised Land. And like Israel, we've been here before. Moses had declared to Pharaoh, through Aaron, "Let my people go!" Eventually, the nation of Israel left Egypt with the wealth of the nation. They were delivered from more than 400 years of captivity. Their deliverance from slavery symbolizes deliverance from the kingdom of darkness and becoming born again. God fed them and gave them water. They had a cloud by day to shade them from the sun and a fire by night to keep them safe and warm. Even their clothing did not wear out. Everything was great until God gave them their next assignment.

When they first came to the Jordan River, God told them to cross and take the land He had promised to their father Abraham. The Promised Land contained seven kingdoms (no doubt symbolic of the seven kingdoms of society). God told them to conquer those kingdoms. They replied, "We liked the last assignment better when You fed and led us, and all we had to do was follow the path." God told them, "Get over there and defeat the nations because their cities, their houses, and their wealth belong to you." (The devil has your stuff too, and it is time to take it back.) However, God could not convince them to do what they did not want to do, so He waited for a generation who was willing to take back the land He had given their forefathers.

In the same way, God has been waiting for a generation of believers who understand their mission and choose to fulfill it. This is that generation: a band of believers who accept the Bible as true, believe that God is able to do what He has said He will do, and are willing to take His Kingdom to the seven kingdoms of earth. By doing so, they give Christ His footstool.

Walking Into Power

Those who "volunteer" to play their parts in what God is doing in the seven mountains will walk into His power to accomplish it.

Keys to Your Kingdom

*I urge you, first of all, to **pray for all people**. As you make your requests, plead for God's mercy upon them, and give thanks. Pray this way **for kings and all others who are in authority**, so that we can live in peace and quietness, in godliness and dignity. This is good and pleases God our Savior, for **He wants everyone to be saved and to understand the truth*** (1 Timothy 2:1-4 NLT).

The broad picture is, *"Pray for all people."* The tighter focus is, *"Pray for kings and all others who are in authority."* Paul was a strategic thinker; he knew that the way to take a kingdom is to capture the king. We are called by God to pray for the transforming Kingdom of God to intersect and invade the lives of those who are in authority in our society. We pray for them because the people who control those mountains control the people under their influence. Until these mountains are taken or conquered for Christ, they are ruled by people who are under the influence of the enemy, who is using them to bring deception and oppression to humankind. We are to pray for the leaders of the kingdoms of culture to come under the influence of God's Kingdom. We want them to become born again, but regardless of their decision, we pray for them to be influenced by God's Kingdom.

Satan never relinquishes his authority over a kingdom until a stronger power demands it. Here is that spiritual law from Jesus' mouth:

> *When a strong man, fully armed, guards his own palace, his goods are in peace. But when a stronger than he comes upon him and overcomes him, he takes from him all his armor in which he trusted, and divides his spoils* (Luke 11:21-22).

The spiritual application of that law is "greater is He who is in you than he who is in the world" (see 1 John 4:4). The reason we have power over the enemy is revealed in Matthew 16:19:

> *And I will give you the **keys of the kingdom of heaven**, and whatever you bind on earth will be bound in heaven, and whatever you loose on earth will be loosed in heaven.*

We have to stop believing and acting as if we are on the losing side. Every revelation God gives us is not meant to merely make us more knowledgeable but to become a *key* that when applied through faith is a means to advance the Kingdom of God in our lives and upon the earth. We have many keys rattling around in our theological collections—keys of healing, casting out demons, love and joy and peace, and more—keys that we need to begin using *outside our churches in our mountains of influence.*

How to Apply Spiritual Keys

When a spiritual truth lights up within us, we have been given a spiritual key. Along with our new understanding, we also receive a spark of faith because according to Romans 10:17, *"Faith comes by hearing...."* That faith is intended to be used to activate the spiritual key to advance God's interest in our lives and on the kingdoms of this world.

Trespassers Will Be Prosecuted!

> *David took the stronghold of Zion (that is, the City of David). ...Then David dwelt in the stronghold, and called it the City of David.... So David went on and became great, and the LORD God of hosts was with him* (2 Samuel 5:7,9-10).

There is only one city that God ever said belonged to Him—Jerusalem—and when David came on the scene, idol worshipers had occupied it for more than 800 years. Many men, good men, before David had tried to take this city from the Jebusites, but none had succeeded. The conquering of this enemy stronghold required a man who was anointed to be both priest and king. The Jebusites were trespassing in a kingdom that rightfully belonged to God, just as satan is trespassing in the seven kingdoms God established: the family mountain, education mountain, religion mountain, government mountain, business mountain, media mountain, and arts and entertainment mountain. Satan has no legal right to those kingdoms and only rules because Christians have abdicated their rightful place and authority in them.

God Is Not Finished With *You!*

Everyone craves a purpose-filled life. And each person's unique purpose contributes to advancing the Kingdom of God. No matter where you are today or what you have been through, God is not finished with your story. Some of the greatest people in the Bible were powerfully used by God when everyone had written them off because they were too young, too damaged, or too old. God, however, was not finished with them, and neither is He finished with you! He has a *reason* for you during this *season* of your life.

According to Revelation 5:10, we too are *"kings and priests to our God; and we shall reign on the earth."* Now that we have been reequipped to conquer the kingdoms of this earth, it is time for us to go **back to** the original purpose given to Adam of bringing God's dominion to earth and thereby bringing to our planet **the future** God intended before He created the universe. This is how the apostle Paul explained it to the Ephesian church:

> *Long ago, even before He made the world, God loved us and chose us in Christ to be holy and without fault in His eyes. His unchanging plan has always been to adopt us into His own family by bringing us to Himself through Jesus Christ.... ...He is so rich in kindness that He purchased our freedom through the blood of His Son, and our sins are forgiven. He has showered His kindness on us, along with all wisdom and understanding. God's secret plan has now been revealed to us; it is a plan centered on Christ, designed long ago according to His good pleasure. And this is His plan: At the right time He will bring everything together under the authority of Christ—everything in heaven and on earth (Ephesians 1:4-5; 7-10 NLT).*

Endnote

1. Myles Munroe, *Kingdom Principles* (Shippensburg, PA: Destiny Image, 2006), 31.

CHAPTER THREE

What Is Your Mountain?

The mountain of influence to which you are called is the place where you will find the job you love, financial success, people you enjoy being with, and ultimate personal fulfillment. Your position in your mountain, the one that God has prepared for you and the one for which you have been prepared, is your "sweet spot," your perfect fit. Not only is it *God's place* where you can most effectively bring to bear His presence and power to affect an area of your culture, but it is also *your place*. If you were a key, the position God called you to would be a lock in which you fit perfectly—the lock on the door of your destiny.

Consider What Life Would Be Like if You Found Your Perfect Place

Finding your perfect place does not mean that your life will be perfect, free of problems and stress, or that you will never do anything else. Rather, it means that you have discovered the great adventure for which you were created. Allow God to put within you a burning desire to know your place in the seven mountains of influence and to reach it, as He put within Caleb.

Caleb, one of the 12 men who spied out the Promised Land for Moses, was assigned to scout the area of Canaan. As you will recall, all the spies except for Caleb and Joshua brought back negative reports that made the people of Israel afraid to enter the Promised Land and take their inheritance. Because of Caleb's positive report, Moses promised to him the area he had scouted:

> *…Surely the land where your foot has trodden shall be your inheritance and your children's forever, because you have wholly followed the* LORD *my God* (Joshua 14:9).

Forty-five years later, after the fearful generation of Israelites was dead and the new, more courageous generation was willing to trust God to help them to take the land, Caleb stood before Joshua and demanded:

> ***Now therefore give me this mountain***, *whereof the* LORD *spake in that day; for thou heardest in that day how the Anakims were there, and that the cities were great and fenced: if so be the* LORD *will be with me, then I shall be able to drive them out, as the* LORD *said. And Joshua blessed him, and gave unto Caleb the son of Jephunneh Hebron for an inheritance* (Joshua 14:12-13 KJV).

Just as Caleb lived with a faith and passion to conquer his mountain, God has given a life's purpose to every man and woman. Your purpose is your position in one or more of the seven mountains of influence. That place is *yours* by divine right; it is your "inheritance" from the Lord.

One of the Most Important Questions You Will Ever Answer Is:

What mountain has God put in your heart to conquer for Him?

Kingdom Now!

The Church has believed for many years that the Kingdom of God Jesus spoke of will come during the Millennium. The Book of Revelation speaks of this age when Jesus will return again to earth and physically reign over the nations of the earth.

In more recent times, some have taken another look at Jesus' teachings and noticed that He said, "The Kingdom is *at hand*" (see Matt. 10:7). To be "at hand" means it must be readily available, within reach. There will no doubt be a millennial kingdom when Jesus will reign forever, but God's Word indicates that *Jesus wants to reign now* in the kingdoms of our culture! We are the "Joshua Generation," a generation of the Church called to possess the kingdoms of culture.

We are not to condemn or try to destroy the mountains of culture because of their present wickedness, corruption, greediness, and evil influence on our world. Instead, we are called to restructure and return them to be the influence on society that was God's intention when He originated them. In other words, God wants to reshape their glory.

When the devil tempted Jesus with the kingdoms of the earth, the Bible says that satan showed Him "*...all the kingdoms of the world **and their glory**"* (Matt. 4:8). Every kingdom of culture has a brilliance that radiates into the culture of that nation and beyond. God wants to return the mountains of culture to their former brilliance to shine like "cities on a hill" radiating truth, purity, and godliness.

Purpose Has Power

You are alive for a *purpose*. The more familiar you are with your purpose, the more power you have over things that would try to steal your life. Take a look at Caleb's conversation with Joshua preceding the request for his mountain:

Now look at me: GOD has kept me alive, as He promised. It is now forty-five years since GOD spoke this word to Moses, years in which Israel wandered in the wilderness. And here I am today, eighty-five years old! I'm as strong as I was the day Moses sent me out. I'm as strong as ever in battle, whether coming or going (Joshua 14:10-11 MSG).

Caleb lived for 45 years in the promise of his purpose and was suspended from the normal aging process because he believed God. There is a reason *you* are alive today, a reason why *you* have not lost your mind, and a reason why the devil could not kill *you*. There is something God promised you, spoke to you, birthed in you, or perhaps something your family was called to do that is unfinished. Your purpose could have been forgotten, or you may have given up on a dream that was God's purpose. Whether you have lost the vision of your Kingdom mandate or never had it, seek Him for it, and God *will* show you your purpose, the reason you are on this planet.

God Is Not Finished With You

Whether you can relate best to the 85-year-old Caleb who demanded his mountain or the young Caleb who was promised his mountain, you have a part in what God is doing today. As long as there is breath in your lungs and your heart is beating, there is a purpose for your life in one of the kingdoms of culture. No one is excluded from what God is doing today for *any* reason.

In the past, the Church has told people that to be "called of God" means to minister as a pastor, evangelist, or missionary. That is wrong! God chooses, anoints, and gifts people for *all* seven mountains of culture. People who are called to be businesspersons, educators, actors, and so forth are just as *chosen*, just as *anointed*, and just as *gifted* by God as those who are called to ministry.

Past outpourings of God have been good things and have had their place. However, we need the kind of revival that produces a *passion* in people to invade the mountains of culture of our cities, states, and nations. We need a revival of the Kingdom of God that transforms the way we do government, education, media, family, business, arts, entertainment, and religion—a revival that actually changes the way people *really* live.

Purpose Ignites Passion

Nehemiah, the cupbearer for the king of Persia, was a man with a great job; he lived like a king. As King Artaxerxes' cupbearer, Nehemiah had an apartment next door to the king's quarters. He ate the king's food and drank the king's wine. Life was good. However, on the day he found his purpose, Nehemiah discovered his passion. That day he went from a guy with a great job to a man with great passion. You have found your purpose when your passion exceeds your pride or concern for your life as Nehemiah's did. This is his story:

> *…It was the month of Kislev in the twentieth year. At the time I was in the palace complex at Susa. Hanani, one of my brothers, had just arrived from Judah with some fellow Jews. I asked them about the conditions among the Jews there who had survived the exile, and about Jerusalem. They told me, "The exile survivors who are left there in the province are in bad shape. Conditions are appalling. The wall of Jerusalem is still rubble; the city gates are still cinders." When I heard this, I sat down and wept. I mourned for days, fasting and praying before the God-of-Heaven.*

> *…At the hour for serving wine I brought it in and gave it to the king. I had never been hangdog in his presence before, so he asked me, "Why the long face? You're not sick are you? Or are you depressed?" That made me all the more agitated. I said, "Long live the king! And why shouldn't I be depressed when the city, the city where all my family is*

buried, is in ruins and the city gates have been reduced to cinders?"
The king then asked me, "So what do you want?" (Nehemiah 1:1-4;
2:1-5 MSG).

It was against the law for a person to take his or her personal problems
into the king's presence; in fact, Nehemiah's sad face was punishable by
death. He could have died for entering the presence of the king wearing his
passion. Yet, instead of the king ending Nehemiah's life when Nehemiah
met his purpose, Nehemiah's passion ignited the king's favor, anointing, and
gifts. And the king of the greatest nation on earth was moved to give him all
that he requested to rebuild the walls of the city of Jerusalem.

Ask Yourself

- What makes you mad?

- What do you love?

- What gives you joy to think about?

- What do you hate?

- What causes indignation to rise in you?

- What would you change if you could?

- What do you think about all the time?

Your passion points to your purpose.

Going Up?

The Bible teaches that God gives each person a special mix of natural and
supernatural gifts both at birth and when he or she is born again. These gifts
are to equip you for your purpose. They determine not only your skills but

also your nature, temperament, and other personal qualities. Discovering and developing your gift mix is necessary for your promotion to that special place for which God created you. Romans 12:6-8 explains what some have called the motivational gifts:

> *Having then gifts differing according to the grace that is given to us, let us use them: if prophecy, let us prophesy in proportion to our faith; or ministry, let us use it in our ministering; he who teaches, in teaching; he who exhorts, in exhortation; he who gives, with liberality; he who leads, with diligence; he who shows mercy, with cheerfulness.*

A modern description of the gifts:

- *Perceivers* (prophets) have a natural discernment that sees to the heart of an issue or a person's motives, and the perceiver desires to reveal the truth.

- *Servants* (ministers) are motivated by a desire to help, and they naturally see what needs to be done, especially to aid others.

- *Teachers* love to do research, study, discover new things, and enjoy communicating their knowledge to others.

- *Exhorters* care for the spiritual needs of others by stimulating, building up, edifying, and cheering up.

- *Givers* are gifted to make money. Money is their friend, giving money excites them, and they are careful with what they have.

- *Administrators* (leaders) can see the bigger picture in a situation, make instant evaluations, and assign steps of action to solve problems.

- People with the gift of *mercy* are focused on the emotional needs of others; they are driven by compassion, love, mercy, and forgiveness.

There are three types of gifts mentioned in the New Testament: the motivational gifts (named above), the power gifts spoken of in First Corinthians

12:7-10 (available to all believers as needed), and the gifts that Jesus gave to build the Church (apostle, pastor, etc.) found in Ephesians 4:11. Your motivational gifts determine your life skills, and your life skills give you an idea about the mountain to which you are called.

Your gifts are your strengths, and they have the power to bring you to the attention of highly placed people, those who have the ability to "make room" for you in the position God intends. Solomon said, *"A man's gift makes room for him, and brings him before great men"* (Prov. 18:16). However, before you can go up, you will have to prove your dedication to use your gift even when it is of no benefit to you and only blesses others. Once you convince the enemy that you are determined to operate in your gift no matter what, he must release you to your destiny.

> Joseph, as a prisoner in an Egyptian jail, volunteered to use his gift to interpret dreams for two men who were merely fellow prisoners, a kind gesture that offered no apparent benefit to him. However, his unselfish act led to his elevation to the top of the government mountain of Egypt (see Gen. 40–41). When you have proven to God that you are a good steward of the gifts He has given, then you become a candidate for the elevator that will take you up to your place in your mountain.

Prophetic Inheritance

God not only calls individuals, but He also calls families. He often gives families a multi-generational assignment to conquer a particular mountain of influence. If a previous generation did not complete that purpose to bring the Kingdom of God to a particular mountain, then a prophetic inheritance and Kingdom mandate remains to be claimed and completed by later generations. That means you may be called to finish an assignment that your ancestors began or should have begun.

Take a thoughtful and prayerful look at your father and mother and their fathers and mothers. Include aunts and uncles. Look as far back as you can in your ancestry for people who had some success in their fields of interest but never pushed through to the top. Look for those who had a significant gift or talent, yet never lived up to their potential. It does not have to be something they did to make a living; it could be something in which they took a special interest. If you do not know very much about your ancestors, ask God to reveal, restore, remind, or introduce you to your prophetic inheritance and multi-generational assignment. Even if you think you may know your generational mandate, ask God for confirmation and illumination. Your assignment may not be exactly what you see in past generations; it could be a modern variation within that same mountain of influence.

Many of God's people should today be at a higher level financially and in other ways. Your ancestor's ceiling should have been your floor. But if the enemy stole an inheritance designed to be passed along to you, then you were probably required to start over from scratch. Perhaps you remember that the Bible says the thief is required to restore seven times what is stolen. Begin requiring reparations for what has been taken; demand that the enemy restore your stolen inheritance sevenfold. When we get it right, we can launch our children and grandchildren into realms of influence that will finish the assignment and make it possible for Jesus to return for His Bride.

The Bridal Gown

...For the time has come for the wedding feast of the Lamb, and His bride has prepared herself. She is permitted to wear the finest white linen. (Fine linen represents the good deeds done by the people of God (Revelation 19:7-8 NLT).

Christ will return for a Bride (His Church) who has arrayed herself with the "glory" of the mountains of influence—a Bride whose "good deeds" include conquering every enemy, fulfilling and enforcing the victory of the Cross, and satisfying the mandate of God to manifest His Kingdom to the nations.

Just as a bride is never dressed by the groom but instead dresses herself, so the Bride of Christ must not wait upon His return to win the world's kingdoms for her. She is a warring bride who must take the provisions of power the Groom provided and go herself into the mountains to gather the glory of those kingdoms with which she will clothe and make herself presentable to the Bridegroom.

Your Place of Authority

You have an ultimate, undefeatable authority in every mountain of influence that God has assigned you to possess. Caleb understood the secret of authority, and that is why he did not fear the giants who inhabited his territory. He knew that the size, skill, and experience of his adversaries did not matter because he had undefeatable authority. If what you are trying to do is not working, then you must ask yourself and God, "Am I in the wrong kingdom?"

Knowing who you are and what you are called by God to do is a vital step in discovering your place of authority, but the all-important step to possessing your authority is realizing who Jesus is and what He did:

>*...He asked His disciples, "Who do people say that the Son of Man is?" And they answered, "Some say John the Baptist; others say Elijah; and others Jeremiah or one of the prophets." He said to them, "But who do you [yourselves] say that I am?" Simon Peter*

*replied," **You are the Christ, the Son of the living God.**" Then Jesus answered him, "**Blessed** (happy, fortunate, and to be envied) **are you**, Simon Bar-Jonah. For flesh and blood [men] have not revealed this to you, but My Father who is in heaven. And I tell you, you are Peter [Greek, Petros—a large piece of rock], and on this rock [Greek, petra—a huge rock like Gibraltar] I will build My church, and **the gates of Hades** (the powers of the infernal region) **shall not overpower it [or be strong to its detriment or hold out against it]. I will give you the keys of the kingdom of heaven**; and whatever you bind (declare to be improper and unlawful) on earth must be what is already bound in heaven; and whatever you loose (declare lawful) on earth must be what is already loosed in heaven"* (Matthew 16:13-19 AMP).

The blessing for recognizing that Jesus is the Son of God and knowing Him intimately is not just receiving eternal life. It is also getting the "keys to the Kingdom of Heaven," which give us the authority to operate successfully in our mountains of influence. Those keys are intended to be used to open the gates of the enemy's strongholds that guard his power over the kingdoms of the earth and to defend our gains in those same kingdoms.

Daniel Foresaw Our Day

*During the reigns of those kings, **the God of heaven will set up a kingdom** that will never be destroyed; no one will ever conquer it. It will shatter all these kingdoms into nothingness, but it will stand forever* (Daniel 2:44 NLT).

But in the end, the holy people of the Most High will be given the kingdom, and they will rule forever and ever. ...As I watched, this horn was waging war against the holy people and was defeating them, until the Ancient One came and judged in favor of the holy people of the Most High. Then **the time arrived for the holy people to take over the kingdom.** *...* **Then the sovereignty, power, and greatness of all the kingdoms under heaven will be given to the holy people of the Most High.** *They will rule forever, and all rulers will serve and obey them* (Daniel 7:18,21-22,27 NLT).

Notice some important things about these prophecies:

- God's purpose is to establish His Kingdom on earth.

- God intends for His people to rule the kingdoms of this world.

- God has judged in favor of His people.

- God's people have an appointed time to take over the kingdoms.

- God will give His people the authority, power, and greatness of the earth's kingdoms.

God "judged in favor of His holy people" based on the victory of the Cross when Jesus completed His work on earth. Now it is time for "the holy people" (you and me) to be an influence of the Kingdom of God into these seven kingdoms.

It really does not matter how uncertain we may be about our capacity to do the job God has set before us; it does not matter how ungodly the kingdoms of our culture have become; and it does not even matter how the rest of the church world regards what we believe we must do. In fact, it isn't about *us* at all. It *is* all about God. God will teach our "hands to make war," just as He did David's (see Ps. 18:34). And as David successfully established the kingdom of Israel over an enemy who was entrenched in the Promised Land, so shall we be successful against our entrenched foe because the battle is not ours but the Lord's.

Pray This Prayer for God's Direction in Your Life

Father God,

I pray that the things You have placed in my heart that have become lost to my consciousness be recalled. I pray that You will give me an understanding of the true passions of my heart and guide me in recognizing my purpose. I pray that in the next few days and weeks, You will reacquaint me with Your purpose for my life, put together the pieces of the puzzle, and help me begin to press into the things You specifically created me to do. I pray that my desire to fulfill Your purpose will burn in my heart and that the words Caleb used will become my battle cry, "Give me my mountain!"

Thank You for hearing and answering the cry of my heart. In the name of Jesus.

I suggest that you pray it until you know your purpose and are possessed with a passion to fulfill it.

In the next chapter, you will discover that each of us has an important part to play in the family kingdom, and you will learn how to tear down family devils that have held you back.

CHAPTER FOUR

Family First

The first realm of influence God created on the earth was the family mountain. Family is, of course, the natural outcome of marriage. When God created a helpmate for Adam, he declared prophetically:

> *"This is now bone of my bones and flesh of my flesh; she shall be called Woman, because she was taken out of Man." Therefore a man shall leave his father and mother and be joined to his wife, and* **they shall become one flesh** (Genesis 2:23-24).

To establish a home where God's purpose for the family can be fulfilled, we must first understand His intentions concerning marriage. Much of it is summed up in the words, "They shall become one flesh." Just as a "house divided against itself cannot stand" (see Matt. 12:25), neither can a marriage be stable unless both husband and wife form a covenant relationship based upon *giving into* the relationship. The enemy's counterfeit definition and the one to which many in our society subscribe is: The better the marriage, the more *you get* from it.

God's Marriage Manual

Many of the requirements for being a godly husband and a godly wife are laid out in Ephesians 5:22-23,28,33:

Wives, submit to your own husbands, as to the Lord. For the husband is head of the wife… So husbands ought to love their own wives as their own bodies; he who loves his wife loves himself. …Let each one of you in particular so love his own wife as himself, and let the wife see that she respects her husband.

This Scripture indicates the roles of a husband and wife in the home: The man should be the leader and lover and the woman the nurturer and respecter. Our culture has gotten it backward and encouraged men to honor and respect their wives and women to love their husbands. Although those things are good, they are not the most needed in a relationship between a man and woman. Unless a man strives to love his wife (as Jesus loves the Church) and a woman to respect her husband (as the Church does Christ), they cannot fulfill each other's deepest needs.

Men were created by God to thrive upon respect and to be willing to die for honor. Women, on the other hand, flourish in an environment of love. Consequently, men need to ask God to teach them how to better love and show their love to their wives, and women need to seek God for how to better admire and show respect to their husbands.

In the environment that love (for a wife) and respect (for a husband) create, God instructs parents to *"Point your kids in the right direction—when they're old they won't be lost"* (Prov. 22:6 MSG) and adds these further guidelines for children and their fathers:

Children, obey your parents in the Lord, for this is right. "Honor your father and mother," which is the first commandment with promise: "that it may be well with you and you may live long on the earth." And you, fathers, do not provoke your children to wrath, but bring them up in the training and admonition of the Lord (Ephesians 6:1-4).

> ## Function of the Family
>
> The family is the place for righteousness to be taught, personal character to be developed and molded, and Kingdom destiny to be discovered and experienced. When we do this correctly, we create the foundation for a life worth living.

Agents on Assignment

The founding of the kingdom of Israel parallels in many ways the founding of God's Kingdom on the earth. Although the enemy cannot know the exact plans of God, he is able to discern times and seasons. When he knows that a new season is beginning, the enemy often tries to kill or render ineffective those whom God intends to use, as he tried to kill Moses and Jesus.

The enemy understands the importance of family, perhaps better than we do, and has given it top priority in his attack upon humankind. When he is able to make a father, mother, or family dysfunctional, he is often successful in limiting the effectiveness of that family and its descendants' ability to fulfill their purpose on the earth.

In each generation, the enemy wages war against children, and the war for the children of this generation is more intense than ever before. He has declared all-out jihad upon this generation because he senses that they are the Joshua Generation, the generation called to fulfill the Church's purpose to bring the Kingdom of God to earth.

> ## You're a Debt Collector, and the Devil Owes You Big Time
>
> Just as the enemy stole from generations of the Israelites by enslaving them through the Egyptians, he has stolen from your ancestors too. And

as the Israelites received their back pay from their oppressors when they asked for it, you have the legal right to demand back from the enemy what was stolen from your past generations. And he must repay with interest, a rate of seven times more (a healthy 700 percent interest). It is time—no, it is past time—for you to make a claim for reparations for all that was stolen from you and from your forefathers. Now is the time to command him to return it all...and with interest!

The children of Israel were brought into the wilderness by God, but it was only intended to be a temporary season of training before they entered the Promised Land. God never meant for a three-week journey in the wilderness to take more than 40 years. Neither is it His intention for the Church to camp for decades on the wrong side of the Jordan in the dispensational belief that "someday" Christ will return to fight and overcome the giants that occupy the inheritance of believers, and after He has fought the battle on their behalf and conquered all the evil giants for them, He will then tenderly place them in their inheritance.

Salvation is symbolized by God's provision for the children of Israel during their time in the wilderness. They had food from Heaven, water from a rock, shade by day, and fire by night. The Church has focused entirely upon the wonderful provisions of salvation. Just as God had more for Israel than the wilderness provisions, He has more for us than the provisions of salvation (as wonderful as they are). God's best for Israel and His best for us is the same: the pursuit of our destiny. They had a destination that "flowed with milk and honey," and we have a destiny in the seven mountains of culture that will be just as sweet and fulfilling.

You're a Special Agent (of the Kingdom of Heaven)

God did not create us to just get saved and then make our own way through life, marking time until we die or Jesus returns. We are on earth as special agents of a higher power, ambassadors of a heavenly realm, sent by God to accomplish an important mission.

You are here on assignment, baby!

Kingdom Living Versus Wilderness Existence

When the Israelites first came to the edge of the Promised Land at the Jordan River, God reminded them that He had given their forefather Abraham the entire area. He told them to cross the Jordan and possess their inheritance. He stated that their inheritance included:

- Kingdoms already created

- Cities already built

- Businesses already flourishing

- Farms already planted

- Vineyards already thriving

- Pastures already filled with herds of animals

- Houses already constructed.

God went on to explain that there were seven nations they had to *dispossess* to get their legacy. They were to drive out, by force, those who were illegally occupying Israel's God-given domain. Israel, however, decided they liked wilderness existence better than battling giants to obtain their inheritance—Kingdom living. They opted for the easy way rather than the risky one that required faith to get all God had promised. This sheds new light on the Scripture in Hebrews 11:6:

> *But without faith it is impossible to please Him, for he who comes to God must believe that He is, and that He is a rewarder of those who diligently seek Him.*

Faith, then, is acting on the belief that God exists, that He "rewards," and that He responds to "those who diligently seek Him." Acting on faith is the proof of our profession of faith.

God had not saved the Israelites to live their lives in the seclusion of the wilderness. Neither has He saved us to settle for being apathetic Christians living isolated lives with a few hours a week of relief from the world in a church service. No! God saved us to be world-transforming agents for His Kingdom.

God's people of today are another Joshua Generation and we once again stand at the River Jordan, a place of decision. (Jordan symbolizes the separation of our salvation experience from our inheritance in the kingdoms of influence in this world.) God is inviting us, sin's former slaves, as He did Egypt's former slaves, to leave our comfortable wilderness existence and cross over into Kingdom living—to find our courage, gifts, and talents and pursue our destinies.

To Miss Our Assignment Is to Miss Our Purpose

The day is coming when every one of us who are Christians will stand before Christ to be judged, not for our sins, but for how well we fulfilled our purpose on the earth. We want to be among those to whom He will say, "Well done, good and faithful servant" (see Matt. 25:23). By accepting our mission in life and ascending to our special places of influence, we will be fulfilling our purpose to bring God's Kingdom to earth, and we will reap a reward in the world to come and in this life for fulfilling our purpose.

Jesus is waiting *for His enemies to be made His footstool* (Heb. 10:13 NIV). The enemies of God were conquered by the work of Jesus. Their right and authority to rule has been taken away. Yet, they remain powerfully active upon the earth because they have not been deposed from their positions of power. And Jesus is "sitting and waiting," waiting for the rightful rulers of earth and of the seven mountains of influence. He is waiting for the redeemed to take their places of power and authority. Christians are commissioned to enforce the victory of the Cross and give glory to God by demonstrating to a world looking for answers—*the Answer*. This answer is what it means for God's Kingdom to live within you.

Demonic Dominions

Every mountain of influence has a stronghold designed to control and oppress humankind and keep Christians from ascending to places of authority. The first obstacle to overcome in conquering the family mountain is discouragement. You might be thinking the same thing countless people have told me: "Pastor, you just don't know my family. We have sexual promiscuity, drug addiction, alcoholism, dysfunctional dads, messed-up mothers, and rebellious kids. I've tried to witness, to live 'the life' in front of them, to bring them to church, but they only get worse. Frankly, I've done all I know to do, and it looks hopeless."

Hopelessness over family situations is the glue that holds us stuck in an attitude of defeat. In fact, we can become so discouraged that when God does show up, all that comes out of us is our pain. That is how Gideon felt when the angel of God appeared to him as he was hiding in a wine vat processing black market wheat.

Imagine a 12-foot angel appearing to you with encouraging words like, "The Lord is with you, mighty man of valor." But you are so discouraged that all you can do is whine, *"...If the Lord is with us, why has all this happened to us? And where are all the miracles our ancestors told us about? ...The Lord has abandoned us and handed us over to the Midianites"* (Judges 6:13 NLT).

Despite his bad beginning, Gideon went home and prepared an offering for God and returned and placed it on a rock. When the angel used his staff to touch the meat and bread that had been drenched in broth, fire flamed up and consumed it, and the angel disappeared. Those fireworks convinced Gideon that the angel actually was from God, but that knowledge, instead of giving him hope, caused a new fear. God's (future) mighty man of valor moaned, *"Oh no! Master, GOD! I have seen the angel of God face-to-face!"* (Judges 6:22 MSG). However, once God had reassured Gideon that he would not die, Gideon was ready to take on his enemy. However, the Lord first required Gideon to go on a covert mission to tear down his father's idols.

Your Daddy's Devils

Before you can display public dominion, you must have private victory.

First, you have to break family or generational curses that hinder you from becoming the person God intended so you can reach your potential.

The greatest demon you will ever face is within your family mountain because demons attach themselves to our family idols. The things that people put in their hearts by their behavior, words, and the devotion of their time or finances become their idols. That "thing" may be a sinful or unhealthy practice or it may be something innocuous, but when it is given a higher place (loved more) than God, it becomes an idol and creates a generational curse:

> *Do not make idols of any kind.... You must never worship or bow down to them, for I, the Lord your God, am a jealous God who will not share your affection with any other god! I do not leave unpunished the sins of those who hate Me, but I punish the children for the sins of their parents to the third and fourth generations* (Exodus 20:4-5 NLT).

How to Create an Idol

Iniquity that is practiced continually goes beyond mere sinning to become idolatry. Generational curses are your weaknesses, sins that seem so instinctive they give the impression that they are impossible to refuse. There is nothing that God cannot set you free from *except* things you will not let go. It is easier for God to set you free than it is for you to receive freedom.

Things we use for gratification and to meet our needs, instead of allowing God to meet them, become our idols—idols infected with demons. Each of us has generational challenges to deal with because of ancestors who made their iniquities into idols, and that is in addition to the idols we craft for ourselves.

Gideon not only tore down his daddy's idols, but he also replaced them with an altar and a sacrifice to God. And that is what we must do with generational idols: Replace them with the "opposite spirit." The opposite spirit of the devil is the Spirit of God, and the fruit of His Spirit contains all the replacements we need. Use love for the idol of hate; patience for the idol of anger; self-control for lust, substance abuse, and the like. There is a fruit of the Spirit to substitute for every family idol. If you will not deal with your unresolved generational issues for yourself, then do it for your kids.

King David had an "eye for the women," and it got him in trouble. You no doubt remember the story of David and Bathsheba and how he had Uriah murdered so he could take Bathsheba for his wife. David repented for that murder and his adultery, but he never dealt with the root issue. His unresolved, unconquered issue became his son's downfall. Solomon, who had more wives than there are days in the year, ended up worshiping the pagan gods of his many women. The wisest guy in the world lost his way because of the generational curse of lust, which he inherited from his father.

Thank God for the Cross!

You can have a new beginning in Jesus Christ. It does not matter if your family history is filled with murderers, scoundrels, drunks, and adulterers. You can come from the weirdest family ever, yet God gives you the opportunity to be different. If God did not offer this get-out-of-jail pass, we would all be perpetual prisoners of generational iniquity with no means of escape. However, every person has a way out through the blood of Jesus, a Helper called the Holy Spirit, and a book to guide you called the Word of God. God can wipe your slate clean and empower you to resist and overcome your daddy's devils. No matter how messed up your family was (or is), you have *no* excuse *not* to change.

The wickedest man in the Bible was Manasseh, the son of King Hezekiah (see 2 Kings 21). His son, Amon, as you might expect, was also a wicked king. However, Manasseh's grandson, Josiah, was one of the most righteous kings ever to rule Israel. He spent his entire life tearing down the idols and demonic structures that his wicked grandfather and father built. He warred until he cleansed Israel of all idolatry. Second Kings 23:25 pays him this tribute:

> *Never before had there been a king like Josiah, who turned to the Lord with all his heart and soul and strength, obeying all the laws of Moses. And there has never been a king like him since* (NLT).

You Can Be Your Family's Josiah!

You can be the one who ends the evil that has been perpetuated in your family for generations: the one who breaks the pattern of divorce, who stops cancers of iniquity, who ends philosophical ideas of demonic origin, who puts a stop to the curse of a particular disease, and who stops self-defeating acts. You can be the one who breaks off every generational curse that has plagued you and your ancestors. First, pray for discernment concerning the demonic forces that afflict you and your family. Next, go to war for yourself and for your descendents.

Claim the Mountain of Your Family

Remember the story of Rahab, the harlot of Jericho who hid the two spies of Israel? They promised her that if she hung a red cord from her window, she and her family would be spared when Jericho fell. She did as she was instructed, hung the red cord, and gathered *all her family* in her home. When the walls of Jericho fell, one small section of wall remained standing, and Rahab and all her family were saved (see Josh. 6:17-25). That thin red line made of cord, symbolizing the shed blood of One who was to come, saved her and her entire family. You, too, have the right and authority to save your *entire family* from eternity without God.

The promise by Paul to the Philippian jailor says it all: *"Believe on the Lord Jesus Christ, and **you will be saved, you and your household"*** (Acts 16:31). Family salvation, however, does not happen automatically. You will have to use your faith, this Scripture, and other Scriptures to wage war for the souls of your family members. But if you will take on this battle, all will be saved. It is time to stop the devil's inroads into your family. It is time to draw a line in the sand and say, "No more! You are not going to torment me or my loved ones again." Take the same position Joshua took when he declared, *"...As for me and my house, we will serve the LORD"* (Joshua 24:15).

To unlock your future and the futures of your children and grandchildren, you must first close the door to the past. Take a moment right now to do what Daniel did. This godliest of men took responsibility for the sins of his father and forefathers and asked God for forgiveness. It is one thing to recognize and criticize the failings of your ancestors, but it is quite another thing to accept accountability before God for their failings and repent on their behalf.

Once you have asked forgiveness with a genuinely contrite heart for your sins, the sins of your sons and daughters, and the sins of your forefathers and received His cleansing, plead the Blood of Christ over your children. Then turn your attention to the enemy and declare that his power over your family is broken, and they are now off limits to him. Fight for your family! Speak deliverance, freedom, and salvation. Refuse to be discouraged or stop believing. Know that eventually, regardless of how sinfully and dysfunctionally they are living today, a new day is coming when they will accept Christ as Savior. Believe that the hand of God will do miracles in your family and P.U.S.H. (Pray Until Something Happens). Push until the Kingdom of God comes to your family mountain!

In the next chapter, we talk about the mountain of religion. This mountain is vital to the taking of the other mountains of culture. However, instead of creating churches that function as arsenals to arm Christians to take their mountains, we've made churches into private clubs featuring all-you-can-eat buffets of spiritual delights. However, things are a-changing...are you?

CHAPTER FIVE

The Church Mountain

The church mountain was not conceived by man; it was God's idea and the creation of Jesus Christ. In fact, Jesus was the first person in the Bible to use the word *church,* as recorded in Matthew 16:16,18:

> *Simon Peter answered, "You are the Christ, the Son of the living God." [Jesus replied,] "...you are Peter [petros], and upon this rock [petra] I will build My church; and the gates of Hades will not overpower it"* (NASB).

When Peter declared who Jesus was—the Christ—Jesus declared who Peter was (or would become)—a large rock who would be foundational to the Church. Then using the Greek word *petra,* which means "a gigantic rock like the Rock of Gibraltar," as a symbol for the huge truth that Jesus is the Christ, He prophesied the beginning of the Church, *"Upon this rock* [not *petros* like Peter but *petra*] *I will build My church."*

What Is the Church?

If 100 people were asked to define the words *church* and *religion,* each would have a different definition. So, to get the real meaning, we must go back to its Creator to discern what Jesus meant. The actual word He spoke that is translated *church* is the Greek word *ecclesia,* which means "called-out ones." It can be no coincidence that the Romans used this same word for the group of indigenous people they selected from each conquered province to take to Rome for training. In Rome, the ecclesiasts sat at the feet of Caesar and the senate to learn the workings and culture of the Roman Empire. After experiencing Roman society and coming to understand the laws and ways of Rome, these members of the ecclesia were returned to their homes to spread Roman culture throughout their provinces.

The ecclesia model is obviously Jesus' intention for the Church. His plan is to summon people (ecclesiasts) from the seven mountains of culture. They are to "sit at His feet" through the ministry of apostles, prophets, pastors, teachers, and evangelists to learn the power and the culture of the Kingdom of Heaven. Then they are to return to (or find) their positions in the seven mountains of culture to bring God's Kingdom to their places of influence.

By using the word *ecclesia,* Jesus was also implying that He intended to take His Kingdom through His Church to the world. Finally, Jesus informed His disciples that the ecclesia (the Church) would be so powerful that even the gates of hell that guarded the kingdoms of earth would not be able to withstand it.

The Purpose of the Church

The Church is ordained to reach the lost and then train Christians in the truth, power, and dynamics of God's Kingdom. It is to equip followers of Christ to return to (or find) their places of influence in the seven mountains of culture to do their part in bringing God's Kingdom to earth.

Jesus did not have the wealth to buy the kingdoms of the world (although God could have provided it). He did not have a large army to send to subdue the nations (although he had legions of angels at His command). Jesus had only the anointing, the plan, and the purpose of God to accomplish His purpose of bringing God's Kingdom to earth. But using the strategy of the ecclesia (the mountain of church), He knew it would be enough.

Even though Jesus could have called legions of angels to subdue the earth and enforce the Kingdom of Heaven upon every person of every nation, His plan was to use people like you and me to spread the Good News of the Kingdom. This is in stark contrast to the dispensational view of the establishment of God's Kingdom on earth which anticipates a failed church, a last-minute airborne rescue, and a divine army to enforce the Kingdom upon the nations.

God's Plan B Is Plan A

When the Church forsakes its *real* purpose (see above) and creates another reason to exist—sometimes called religion—it loses its influence and relevance and is no longer important to the culture. God, however, does not invest His presence, power, and blessing into plans and projects that diverge from His original intention for the Church to train and equip ecclesiasts.

Throughout the decades, the Church has misunderstood what Jesus meant when He named His Church the "called-out ones," and it has connected that term with Matthew 22:14, *"For many are called, but few are chosen."* The Church has reached some erroneous conclusions from this verse and used them to:

1. Excuse our inability to enlarge the Church.

2. Provide a false sense of success for our failure to "disciple nations."

3. Create a false pride that we are the "chosen ones," the few who were spiritual enough to see the truth.

Jesus' statement that "many are called, but few are chosen" did not mean any of those things. It was an adaptation of a term used by the Roman army.

When Jesus spoke those words, they were like a parable to His hearers who understood His reference.

For more than 500 years, the army of Rome was the greatest army the world had known. They conquered every land and won every campaign they undertook. You may have heard the boast reportedly spoken by Julius Caesar: *"Veni, vidi, vici"* (meaning "We came, we saw, we conquered"). Because of its proud history of successful campaigns, being accepted into the Roman army was the greatest of honors and the highest status one could attain. Consequently, most men of the Roman Empire longed to be in a Roman legion. Each spring a call went out for every man 16 to 46 years old with an interest in joining the army to come to a Campus Martius, outside Rome, where their worthiness would be tested—in other words, "many were called."

Every activity useful to combat was practiced on this massive field that lay alongside the Tiberias River: swimming, climbing, running, wrestling, carrying heavy weights, fencing, throwing the javelin, and more. Sergeants from the various legions and their cohorts worked with the would-be recruits while the officers observed. They were looking for people who showed dedication, determination, and the ability to learn the skills required of a Roman soldier. When a man had proved himself worthy of acceptance into the army, someone would whisper in his ear, "You're chosen." Hence, "many were called but few were chosen."

In Matthew 22:14, Jesus was telling people that within the Church everyone is called to go into the mountains of society and find greatness and that the Church is intended to be the place of training for taking kingdoms and conquering the mountains of family, business, church, government, education, media, and arts and entertainment. To become chosen, one must be like the men who were determined to join the Roman army—they must have the passion, desire, and determination to fulfill their destinies. Everyone can be chosen!

There are only two overarching realms of governance on the earth, and everyone belongs to one or the other: God's Kingdom or the kingdom of satan. God wants humankind to be free from sin and the bondage to satan's kingdom, and He created the church mountain to inform humankind that they now have a choice. When God sent Moses to liberate the children of Israel, he preached a short sermon to Pharaoh: "Thus says the Lord, 'Let My people go!'" Then God caused ten plagues that challenged the authenticity of Egypt's demon-inspired deities. Finally, God told the families of Israel to sacrifice a perfect lamb and place its blood on the doorposts of their homes. That night, the death angel visited Egypt but passed over every home covered by the blood. Pharaoh and his people were not so fortunate. Finally, Pharaoh told them to "get out" (see Exod. 5–13). That event is a portrait of God's plan to set humankind free from the kingdom of satan. By applying the innocent blood of the Lamb of God, we are set free from sin and satan. However…

Don't Leave Empty Handed

You should not leave any season of your life without the secret treasure that is buried somewhere in the walls, the floor, or the surrounding areas of your place of captivity. Just as the Hebrews plundered the wealth of Egypt when they left, we too are to get all we have coming. During the span of one day, the richest nation on earth became the poorest and the poorest became the richest nation, and He will do the same for you.

Coaches for Conquest

When God told Israel to enter the Promised Land and dispossess its inhabitants of their control of the land, He created a picture of His plan for the last-day Church. And when Christ departed the earth, He left us "gifts" intended to equip us for dominion:

> *He who descended is the very One who ascended higher than all the heavens, in order to fill the whole universe. It was* **He who gave** *some to be apostles, some to be prophets, some to be evangelists, and some to be pastors and teachers,* **to prepare God's people for works of service, so that the body of Christ may be built up** (Ephesians 4:10-12 NIV).

In this verse 10, Paul reveals the Son's purpose in coming to earth *"…that He [His presence] might fill all things (the whole universe, from the lowest to the highest)"* (AMP). Now that Christ resides in Heaven, His presence on earth is the Body of Christ. Skipping past the statement of the gifts Jesus gave, verse 12 says that Christ gave those gifts for the purpose of preparing Christians for "works of service." What could your service be but the fulfilling of your God-appointed destiny?

The building up of the Body of Christ refers to strengthening and equipping God's people to serve Him and His Kingdom. So it becomes clear that the gifts Christ gave to His followers are especially anointed people called apostles, prophets, evangelist, pastors, and teachers who are intended to mentor and coach Christians to carry out their purpose. For centuries, the Church has had an introverted belief that the ministry gifts were merely meant to help Christians become more mature and to encourage them to remain faithful until Jesus returns. Now we are returning to understand that the Church's *real* purpose is to equip Christians for their callings in the mountains of culture.

In the very next verses, Paul explains what the Body of Christ will look like when we all "grow up." (The parts important to understanding the function of the church mountain are put in boldface.):

> [This will continue] *until we come to such unity in our faith and knowledge of God's Son that* **we will be mature and full grown**

*in the Lord, measuring up to the full stature of Christ. Then we will no longer be like children, forever changing our minds about what we believe because someone has told us something different or because someone has cleverly lied to us and made the lie sound like the truth. Instead, we will hold to the truth in love, **becoming more and more in every way like Christ**, who is the Head of His body, the church. **Under His direction, the whole body is fitted together** perfectly. As **each part does its own special work**, it helps the other parts grow, so that **the whole body is healthy and growing** and full of love* (Ephesians 4:13-16 NLT).

Unpacking Ephesians 4:13-16

- The fivefold ministry gifts, mentioned in earlier verses of Ephesians 4, are intended to help us *"grow in every way"* and become what Christ intended, purveyors of the Kingdom.

- *"Maturing in the Lord"* means measuring up to the *"full stature of Christ."* His standard is our mission to disciple nations by taking the Kingdom of God to each nation's mountains of influence.

- The Body of Christ will *"fit together perfectly"* as each of us find and pursue our unique anointing, gifts, and calling to do our *"special work."*

- When we find our places of influence and help others to find theirs, the Body of Christ will be *"healthy and growing."*

The most important mountain of culture is the family mountain. But the second-most important is the church mountain because God wants His people to understand what Christ can do for them and be trained and equipped to do for Christ what He intended.

Although it has been said in previous chapters, it needs repeating again and again until we really get it: We have preached the Gospel of Christ but not the Gospel Christ preached, the Gospel of the Kingdom. Paul preached the Gospel of the Kingdom while in prison in Rome. Acts 28:30-31 says that he:

*...Received all who came to him, **preaching the kingdom of God** and teaching the things which concern the Lord Jesus Christ with all confidence, no one forbidding him.*

What Is the Kingdom of God?

Although one day it will be an actual kingdom, the Kingdom of God today is the reign of Christ in the hearts of men and women. That reign releases His unique plan for their lives—a purpose that will give them an "abundant life" and manifest God's purpose on earth. It is a return to God's original intention for humankind to "have dominion" over all the earth as stewards or "caretakers" for its Creator and Owner, God.

The Paraclete Advantage

Here is a very brief summary of what happened about 2.000 years ago from Heaven's standpoint: The Son of God came to earth, died for the cause, went to hell, defeated satan, took back the keys of earthly authority, rose from the dead, returned to Heaven where His blood sacrifice for the sins of all mankind was accepted, and was told by God to take a seat. Then God sent the Holy Spirit to earth.

We have talked about why Jesus did not immediately return to set up His Kingdom on earth, but let us now ask: Why was the Holy Spirit sent to earth instead? He was sent to be the general in charge of God's campaign to usher His Kingdom into the earth and set up the return of Christ.

*For the **kingdom of God is** not a matter of eating and drinking, but of **righteousness, peace and joy in the Holy Spirit*** (Romans 14:17 NIV).

The Kingdom of God on the earth is now under the governance of the Third Person of the Trinity, the Holy Spirit. The Church works under Him in submission and cooperation, empowered by the Holy Spirit to extend the Kingdom of God.

We have misunderstood the Holy Spirit's mission on earth. We have made it a tongue, a prophecy, a giggle, or an emotion and thought that His role outside the Church was to draw people to salvation and convict of sin. He does indeed do those things, but His primary role is far bigger; it is to empower Christians to bring God's Kingdom to the nations. Jesus explains the vital importance of the Holy Spirit to the Church in John 14:12,16:

*I assure you, most solemnly I tell you, if anyone steadfastly believes in Me, he will himself be able to **do the things that I do**; and he will do even greater things than these, **because I go to the Father.... And I will ask the Father, and He will give you another Comforter** [Paraclete] **(Counselor, Helper, Intercessor, Advocate, Strengthener, and Standby)**, that He may remain with you forever* (AMP).

When the Church withdraws from the world, it loses its relevance to society, as we have already stated. But what if:

- The best businesspeople came out of the Church?
- The best politicians came from the Church?
- The best musicians, artist, educators, media people, etc., came out of the Church?

When the best and the brightest of the seven mountains of influence come from the church, our buildings will not be able to contain all who will flock there to learn their secrets.

What Is the Paraclete Advantage?

Christians have within them the Holy Spirit, who is their divine Counselor, Helper, Intercessor, Advocate, and Strengthener. Plus, they also have at their disposal the power gifts: the working of miracles, prophecy, discerning of spirits, different kinds of tongues, the interpretation of tongues, words of knowledge, words of wisdom, faith, and gifts of healing. Obviously, Christians have an edge over non-Christians in the workplace—or they should. It is time for us to begin using the "Paraclete Advantage"—the power of the Holy Spirit who already resides within us to fulfill our purpose and regain positions of influence within the mountains of culture.

Stronghold of the Church Mountain—Pride

Many in the church mountain have pride for the beauty of their church buildings, pride in their worship services, pride in their pastors, pride in their theology, pride in their spiritual giftedness, and pride in the belief that they have "the truth" and others are less spiritual or deceived. We can have pride in so many things, and yet not be doing anything that *really* makes a difference in our world. Pride can be a problem for anyone in any mountain of influence and must be dealt with before it becomes a downfall. For those whose assignment is the church mountain, pride will keep you from your purpose of bringing the Kingdom of Heaven to earth. Only the humble can possess the Kingdom of God, and only the meek are allowed to receive the earth for their inheritance:

> *Blessed are the poor in spirit, for theirs is the kingdom of heaven. ...*
> *Blessed are the meek* [or the teachable], *for they shall inherit the earth* (Matthew 5:3,5).

If we choose to continue in pride, the Bible warns: *"Pride goes before destruction, and a haughty spirit before a fall"* (Prov. 16:18). Are you especially gifted and talented? Then be on guard, because those who have the greatest gifts and the largest capacity—regardless of their mountain—are the ones most tempted with pride.

For those who believe they are too spiritual to develop the sin of pride, consider what lay at the root of the fall of the wisest, most anointed, and most beautiful angel that God created. He stood continually in God's very presence, yet fell from his place because of *pride:*

> *How you are fallen from heaven, O Lucifer, son of the morning! How you are cut down to the ground, you who weakened the nations! For you have said in your heart: "I will ascend into heaven, I will exalt my throne above the stars of God; I will also sit on the mount of the congregation on the farthest sides of the north; I will ascend above the heights of the clouds, I will be like the Most High." Yet you shall be brought down to Sheol, to the lowest depths of the Pit* (Isaiah 14:12-15).

Smallness Is the Key to Greatness

If you want a promotion from the Lord, then James has a word of wisdom for you, *"**Humble yourselves** in the sight of the Lord, and He will lift you up"* (James 4:10).

Peter added: *"Therefore **humble yourselves** under the mighty hand of God, that He may exalt you in due time"* (1 Pet. 5:6).

Do you see it? We have the capacity to take on an opposite spirit to pride; we can humble ourselves. However, according to Solomon, if we fail to be humble, "destruction" and "a fall" lie ahead. Yet, by practicing humility, we can put ourselves in a place of favor "under the mighty hand of God" for a timely promotion.

The Church, unfortunately, is accomplished at judging the sins of the flesh in others but blind to the greater sin of pride within itself. Satan specializes in tempting us in ways that we do not recognize as sin, and pride is the most subtle weapon in his arsenal. The thing that keeps people in unbreakable bondages is almost always pride. Do you want to be great? Then consider Jesus' advice: *"The greatest person in the kingdom of heaven is the one who makes himself humble like this child"* (Matt. 18:4 NCV).

We bust pride by making ourselves worship, being passionate in worship, submitting one to another, and submitting to those God has placed over us in positions of authority. When the Church conquers pride, we will establish the Kingdom of God in the church mountain in a powerful way. Pride is the enemy of your destiny, regardless of your mountain.

You Know You Have Pride When You:

- Are not teachable.

- Cannot submit to those in authority.

- Have a hard time worshiping.

- Are hypercritical or judgmental.

- Have a condescending attitude toward others (especially those of other races and religions).

- Are self-righteous.

The Church is vital to God's plan as the place of anointing and equipping to bring His Kingdom to earth. You can see your purpose and know your gifts, and yet you will not be able to fulfill your destiny without the equipping and anointing that comes by the Holy Spirit through the Church. (The Church is God's way of establishing His Kingdom on earth, and the only way a person can become empowered to fulfill his or her God-given destiny.)

The world has yet to see anything like the last-day Church, the Church of the Joshua Generation.

Next we talk about the mountain of business and finance. Those in the business world are just as called and anointed for the business mountain as a pastor in the church mountain. Yet, to operate in that kind of power and anointing, many will have to change their attitudes about work. A job in business cannot be viewed as merely a source of income for the things we enjoy doing; it is our divine calling and purpose, the place God wants to use to promote us to positions of wealth and influence.

CHAPTER SIX
The Mountain Kingdom of Business

If you are working now or plan to work in business or finance in the future, your job is more than the "daily grind," something you have to endure. It is a Kingdom calling, God's assignment to take a mountain for His Kingdom. To boost you to your place of blessing and favor in the mountain of business, God expects you to bring three things to the business kingdom: the influence of God, the example of Christlikeness, and the godly stewardship of wealth.

God Himself is the One who created the first business. Yes, God is a businessman too. His is a family business, so God entrusted it to His son, Adam, and gave to him the authority and guidelines to run it successfully. Because God created Adam's workplace, the Garden of Eden, before He made Adam, we can say that He created man's occupation before making the man. Adam's job caused him to recognize his need for a helpmate, which prompted God to make Eve. Although most of us think of paradise as a place of leisure where no work is required, man worked in God's paradise. According to Genesis 2:8 and 15, humankind was created to work:

The LORD God planted a garden eastward in Eden.... Then the LORD God took the man and put him in the garden of Eden to tend [cultivate, work it] and keep it.

Survive? You Were Created to Thrive

From the beginning, it was God's intention for men and women to be blessed. In the very first words God spoke to man, He did not curse man but blessed him:

God spoke: "Let us make human beings in Our image, make them reflecting Our nature so they can be responsible for the fish in the sea, the birds in the air, the cattle, and, yes, Earth itself, and every animal that moves on the face of Earth." God created human beings; He created them godlike, reflecting God's nature. He created them male and female. God blessed them: "Prosper! Reproduce! Fill Earth! Take charge!" (Genesis 1:26-28 MSG).

The first words Jesus spoke in His most famous message were "Blessed are..."; then He went on to tell us eight ways to be blessed in the sermon called the Beatitudes (see Matt. 5:3-11). The apostle John's greeting to a friend mentions an important key to receiving God blessing of financial prosperity and good health—he calls it soul prosperity: *"Beloved, I pray that you may prosper in all things and be in health, just as your soul prospers"* (3 John 1:2). Both financial and health prosperity require that our souls be restored to the image of God, in which they were created.

Hi Ho, Hi Ho, Off to ? We Go

A society or individual that loses the work ethic will experience an economic decline. When the influence of the Gospel dwindles in a nation, other philosophies enter. One idea that has gained traction in America is the belief that people "deserve" certain things even if they do not work.

The Bible, however, speaks very clearly to this in Second Thessalonians: *"If anyone will not work, neither shall he eat"* (3:10). This was directed primarily to men as providers and protectors of their families. It is saying that no one, neither the Church nor the government, is responsible for providing for someone who does not work. The Message Bible paraphrase of this verse is even more graphic:

> *...Refuse to have anything to do with those among you who are lazy and refuse to work the way we taught you. Don't permit them to freeload on the rest. We showed you how to pull your weight when we were with you, so get on with it* (2 Thessalonians 3:6-7).

As God has restored to the Church the knowledge that He wants His people to prosper, some have believed they could sit on their couches and command their mailboxes to be stuffed full of money. Obviously, it does not work that way. You cannot use your faith to leap over the requirement of work and yet prosper. To reap you must sow your efforts to give God something with which to work.

Master Plan for Prosperity

When God was instructing Joshua in how to be successful at his job of leading Israel into the Promised Land, He gave some important keys we can all use for success. God instructed Joshua:

> *Only be strong and very courageous, that you may observe to do according to all the law which Moses My servant commanded you; do not turn from it to the right hand or to the left, that you may prosper wherever you go. This Book of the Law shall not depart from your mouth, but you shall meditate in it day and night, that you may observe to do according to all that is written in it. For then you will make your way prosperous, and then you will have good success* (Joshua 1:7-8).

God's Rules for Success and Prosperity

We can extract from these verses keys to success that will work for you too.

1. *"Be strong and very courageous"*—Fearlessly pursue your dreams and purpose.

2. *"Observe to do according to all the law"*—The Bible is your handbook for business success

3. *"This Book of the Law shall not depart from your mouth...meditate in it"*—One way to keep your mind focused on God's truth is by confessing it with your mouth and another is to meditate or mull the Word over in your mind.

4. *"You will make your way prosperous"*—When you do the above, your success is now up to you. Stop begging for a blessing; God has given you the key to success in His Word.

5. *"Then you will have good success"*—When God's truth is put in a place of prominence in your life as your most treasured of beliefs, God promises that you will conquer your promised land, the mountain to which you are called.

God was saying to Joshua that His Word blesses everything it goes into, and when it goes into you, it will bless you. The Book of Psalms explains it like this:

> *Blessed is the man who walks not in the counsel of the ungodly, nor stands in the path of sinners, nor sits in the seat of the scornful; but **his** [the blessed man's] **delight is in the law of the LORD, and in His law he meditates day and night**. He shall be like a tree planted by the rivers of water, that brings forth its fruit in*

*its season, whose leaf also shall not wither; and **whatever he does shall prosper*** (Psalm 1:1-3).

You have to love that last phrase, *"whatever he does shall prosper."* Why not make it your goal to enter into a season when everything you do is blessed?

Solomon has more sage advice concerning success:

Roll your works upon the Lord [commit and trust them wholly to Him; He will cause your thoughts to become agreeable to His will, and] so shall your plans be established and succeed (Proverbs 16:3 AMP).

This is how that Scripture works:

- *"Roll your works upon the Lord"*—This means pray with faith, asking for God's help in business situations where you need wisdom.

- *"He will cause your thoughts to become agreeable to His will"*—God promises to give you His wisdom for your projects by aligning your thoughts to His. Instead of having thoughts birthed out of your experience or deductive reasoning, you can have God's thoughts and that will establish your plans for certain success.

God's Purpose for Those in Business

God expects you, as His child, to take up the family business and to be as Jesus would be if He was in your mountain. That means you are to advance His Kingdom through:

1. Displaying Christlikeness, which is another way of saying, *"Be conformed to the image of His Son..."* (Rom. 8:29).

2. Deploying your influence to forward the purpose of God's Kingdom.

3. Stewarding wealth, both your personal wealth and the wealth you manage for others, in a faithful and righteous way.

There are already Christians high in the mountain of business and other mountains, but many of them are not using their influence for God's Kingdom, and they are unaware that God expects it of them. Many of them are good Christians, but they are not good ambassadors for the Kingdom. They have not understood God's purpose for their promotions into positions of influence. When we fail to utilize our promotions for God's Kingdom, we have wasted our advancement.

The Orphan Girl Who Rescued a Nation

Regardless how bad your life may look now, you have reason to hope for things to improve. The Bible is full of stories about underdogs who achieved greatness in their mountains of culture with His help. One of the most famous of these stories is of an orphan girl who, out of hundreds of thousands of girls in the Babylonian empire, was chosen to be queen (see Esther 2). No one knew that she was Jewish because no one asked, but everyone was drawn to her because she had a humble spirit (virtuous and godly).

It is unlikely that Esther was the most beautiful woman they interviewed, had the best hairdo, was the most perfectly made up, or was wearing the most fashionable clothing. Yet when the king met her, he was as fascinated with her inner beauty as he was with her outer beauty. Even the world appreciates and values the qualities that only Christlike people can display.

You will recall that King Ahasuerus' first wife, Vashti, was the most beautiful woman in the entire kingdom. However, when he called for her to show her off as his most precious possession, she arrogantly declined (see Esther 1:10-12). She had great beauty but did not know its purpose and turned her back when the king called. She failed to understand that the beauty she possessed was not solely for her to admire in the mirror; her gift had a purpose that was beyond her. We can learn from Vashti that when we are promoted to positions of power and influence, we must not turn our back on our King and make our gift and position all about us.

Every gift and ability we have was given to us for a mission and calling. Our gifts and our calling are irrevocably tied together. Consequently, when we do not fulfill our calling, we have wasted our gifts regardless of the degree of success we may gain in the world. Our goal must be to find the will and plan of God for every season of our lives and for each of our gifts. That means that even horrible seasons have a Kingdom purpose. In addition, we have to unplug from the world's viewpoint that to accomplish anything worthwhile we have to have money. We are ambassadors of God's Kingdom! And the lowest person in His Kingdom has more power than the wealthiest person in the world.

You probably remember the rest of Esther's story. She risked her position and even her life to save the Jews, who were living in captivity throughout the Babylonian Empire. She not only successfully saved her people, but she also defeated the enemy of her people, and the king of the greatest empire of that day loved, adored, and celebrated her. This is a perfect example of the blessing and reward one receives for seeking first God's Kingdom, as Jesus said in Matthew 6:33: *"But seek **first the kingdom** of God and His righteousness, and all **these things shall be added** to you."*

"Seek first the Kingdom" are words to live by for those who would prosper in the mountain of business and finance.

Buried Assets

After graduating from Bible college, I went to work as an associate pastor at a church that could not afford to pay me. So, to provide for my new bride and myself, I had to work a factory job—and I hated it. As a pastor's son who had grown up attending Christian schools and then went to Bible school, I had been raised in fairly sheltered environment, so I hated every hour that I worked in the factory because I thought I should be at the church doing something "spiritual." Every evening I came home and fell into the arms of my new bride and complained about how much I despised my job. I expressed to her my astonishment and dismay at the conduct of the people with whom I worked, "They actually cuss, they get drunk at lunch time, they flirt, and I feel like Lot in Sodom. It's just horrible, honey. My soul is vexed beyond belief."

After about six months of listening to this every day, my wife had a little talk with me. "Sweetheart," she said sweetly, "*maybe* God has something for you in this job. *Maybe* if you changed your attitude and discovered why He put you there, *maybe* He would let you leave." I was soon to discover that the way out of a bad season is to pass that season's test. Do not worry about failing. God will not allow you to be unsuccessful; He will keep you in the same situation until you "get it."

The next day, I went to work early, at 5:00 A.M., and walked around the huge building passionately praying for a move of God. Soon I started a Bible study, and before long there were 40 to 60 people attending. They were all getting saved, and we were having revival. Then suddenly, for no apparent reason and without my having the education or the experience to justify it, I was promoted into upper management (but I continued my Bible studies). When you get the right agenda, the Kingdom agenda, God will get you promoted because you have made your job about Him rather than about yourself.

When I was able to quit that job about a year later, they begged me to stay. I left feeling that I had seized my opportunity and completed my assignment. So, never leave until you first win the victory. But if you do jump ship, never fear. God will put you back into exactly the same situation somewhere else. Every negative situation in which you find yourself has a Kingdom purpose hidden within it, a hidden asset, and you must find that "pearl of great price" to graduate to your next assignment.

Show Me the Money

For decades, the Church believed that poverty was more virtuous than wealth. For the most part, they based that doctrine on First Timothy 6:10:

For the love of money is a root of all kinds of evil, for which some have strayed from the faith in their greediness, and pierced themselves through with many sorrows.

However, throughout His Word, God declares that He will give you money, resources, provisions, and prosperity if you will love *Him*. This Scripture warns of the opposite side of the coin, making money your *first* love. The love of money or greed is the source for much of the evil on the earth, and those who love money more than God *will* cause themselves much sorrow.

First Timothy 6:17-18 adds:

Command those who are rich in this present age not to be haughty, nor to trust in uncertain riches but in the living God, who gives us richly all things to enjoy. Let them do good, that they be rich in good works, ready to give, willing to share.

This Scripture is for everyone who lives in America. You may not think of yourself as rich, but even the poorest among us have a higher standard of living than 90 percent of the world. We are the wealthiest nation to ever exist, and even in recession, we are the most blessed nation on the planet. Consequently, God is speaking to *us* when He commands, "Be rich in good works, ready to give, willing to share."

Golden Rules for Getting More Gold

*He who is **faithful in what is least is faithful also in much**; and he who is unjust in what is least is unjust also in much* (Luke 16:10).

RULE 1: The way to getting more in the future is to be faithful with what you have today. God never asks us to give what we do not have.

He never holds us accountable for what is not ours. However, when we submit what we *do have* to God and give as He has directed in tithes, to missions, and to help the poor, God will promote us. We cannot wait for "our ship to come in" before we are obedient. God will not let us go to the next level until we have proven faithful on this level. The fact is, the higher the income, the harder it is to tithe. I once pastored a church with 150 millionaires, but only a few actually tithed. The rest merely "tipped" God.

> *He sought God in the days of Zechariah, who had understanding in the visions of God; and as long* **as he sought the LORD, God made him prospe**r (2 Chronicles 26:5).

RULE 2: God wants you to seek Him *first,* rather than seeking first wealth and prosperity, and when you do so, you become a candidate for prosperity.

> *And you shall* **remember the LORD** *your God, for it is He* **who gives you power to get wealth,** *that He may establish His covenant which He swore to your fathers, as it is this day* (Deuteronomy 8:18).

RULE 3: God will give you natural and supernatural help to become wealthy when you "remember" Him. This means you must keep yourself continually in a right and intimate relationship with God and be faithful to His expectations and requirements concerning money and wealth.

Greed—The Demonic Stronghold Over Business

It should come as no surprise that greed is satan's stronghold in the mountain of business and finance, but have you considered that being greedy does not require being rich? You do not have to have lots of money to love it or horde what you do have. Actually, people with little who ignore God's requirements concerning money demonstrate the same greed as the millionaire who only "tips" God.

> *The world of the generous gets larger and larger; the world of the stingy gets smaller and smaller. The one who blesses others is abundantly blessed; those who help others are helped* (Proverbs 11:24-25 MSG).

When capitalism loses the underpinning of the Christian ethos and ethic, it becomes a medium for greedy men and women to plunder society. In recent times, we have seen the plundering of this country by modern-day business pirates. We need God back in Wall Street and back in the mountain of business. The truth is, capitalism easily becomes abused by dishonesty and greed unless it is anchored by the morality of the Judeo-Christian ethic.

Look at Russia. When they came out of the godless governmental system of communism, they had no understanding of Christian morality. Consequently, today Russian capitalism is run by gangsters and is the most predatory and dishonest economic system the developed world has ever seen. Socialism, however, with all its promises, is no better. It is even more costly to individual freedom and produces the same bad results. Greed cannot be effectively controlled by government; it can only be harnessed by Christlikeness.

How to Know If You Are Greedy

The litmus test for greed is simple. You can grade your greed by the answer to a single question: *Do you give?* If you are not giving tithes and offerings as the Lord has commanded, then no matter what your excuse, you are greedy. However, the weapon for killing the beast of greed is simple—giving.

Make greed become your trigger to give. Every time it raises it ugly head to whisper in your mind, "You can't afford to give in this offering," defy it and give something anyway. You overcome evil with good (by choosing the opposite spirit). So slay the dreadful monster of greed.

When a minister talks about giving, some people automatically tune out because to them it sounds self-serving. (Many ministers, including me, give more than the required 10 percent of their incomes to God.) Consider this: God will meet my needs and those of everyone in ministry with or without the gifts of any person. *We do not need for you to give—you need for you to give* to qualify for the blessings God has stored up for you and to avoid the curse of "poverty," which results from "withholding" from God:

> *Give, and it will be given to you: good measure, pressed down, shaken together, and running over will be put into your bosom. For with the same measure that you use, it will be measured back to you* (Luke 6:38).

If you will, *"Honor the Lord with your capital and sufficiency [from righteous labors] and with the firstfruits of all your income,"* the result is *"... Your storage places* [will] *be filled with plenty, and your vats shall be overflowing with new wine"* (Prov. 3:9-10 AMP).

That which you give to God does not leave your life but goes into your future to produce a harvest. By giving, you are not stuffing money down a "black hole," as the enemy would tell you, but you are sowing into your future. When you are generous to God according to *your resources*, He is generous to you according to *His resources*.

The Dividend of Contentment

Our culture is built on seducing people into desiring things they must go into debt to obtain. Then greedy banks and financial institutions charge inflated interest rates to compound our indebtedness. The result can be that most of our income goes to pay, many times over, for something we should have waited until we had the cash to purchase.

> *But godliness with* **contentment is great gain**. *For we brought nothing into the world, and we can take nothing out of it. But if we have food and clothing, we will* **be content** *with that. People who want to get rich fall into temptation and a trap and into many foolish and harmful desires that plunge men into ruin and destruction* (1 Timothy 6:6-9 NIV).

There was a time when I drove a clunker of a car. It constantly had things go wrong with it, and I hated that car. One day the Lord rebuked me for my attitude of ingratitude. He started showing me that I should be content with what I had. So every day I worked on changing my mind about that car, and instead of cursing it, I would say with all the sincerity I could muster, "Thank You, Lord, for my nice car." From that day forward, I never had another problem with that car and even came to enjoy driving it. The Bible teaches that contentment rests in the knowledge that God loves you and will never go away from you or give up on you:

> *Make sure that your character is free from the love of money, being content with what you have; for He Himself has said,* "**I will never desert you, nor will I ever forsake you**" (Hebrews 13:5 NASB).

The One Sin God Will Not Overlook

When the children of Israel were beginning to take their inheritance in the Promised Land, they enjoyed a great success at Jericho. Confident that they could take the lesser cities of the area, they sent a smaller military force to the small city of Ai. However, they suffered a devastating loss. Only a few of the enemy defeated Israel's larger force. When Joshua heard of their defeat, he fell on his face before the Lord and asked, "Why?" And (I am paraphrasing) God answered, "There is sin in the camp" (see Josh. 7).

You may already know this story and what happened to cause God to not only withhold His blessing from the Israelites' campaign but to actually curse it to failure. We will talk about that later, but first consider that in a camp of more than 2 million people there had to be a lot of sinning going on—people lying, cheating, stealing, and committing adultery. God, however, was giving them grace to ask forgiveness and make things right for their sins. However, everything came to a screeching halt because of *one sin*. God refused to overlook one man's sin of greed. Think of it: one man who committed one sin out of millions of people.

God had decreed that all the wealth of Jericho was to be devoted to Him, a tithe on what He was about to give them in the Promised Land. It was the firstfruits principle in operation. One greedy guy kept a little silver, a little gold, and a few expensive clothes, and for this seemingly minor theft of the tithe, God judged an entire nation. (That is something to consider when you think about whether you can afford to write a tithe check.)

In the New Testament when the church in Jerusalem was growing exponentially, God interrupted everything and brought it to a halt over *one sin* of one couple, the sin of greed. Ananias and his wife, Sapphira, had pledged to this growing church (perhaps to its building fund) the proceeds from the sale of a property. God did not require or need all or any of their money, but they had promised all the money to God. Ananias, wanting to take some of the money for himself, lied to the apostles and to God about the amount they received from the sale. That lie produced by greed cost him and his wife everything, including their lives (see Acts 5:1-10). Obviously, God takes the sin of materialism very seriously, but it is not because He does not want you to have stuff; it is because He does not want stuff to have you.

To ascend the mountain of business and finance, you will have to beat the beast of greed to death. The way to do that is to submit *everything* you have to God. I am not suggesting that you give everything away as Jesus told the "rich young ruler" who came to Him in Matthew 19:16 asking what he should do to have eternal life. However, you must be willing to give everything you value to God should He ask for it. That is what it means to love God more than money. Twice, my wife and I have given away everything we had. We did it because we felt that God wanted us to and believed that it would create a new season and a new harvest for us.

A Now Word From God

As I preached this sermon to my church in the spring of 2010, God told me that He is creating a new world economy. He said that He wants His people to be on the cutting edge of what He is doing and to have access to the wealth that He is going to create around the world.

To align yourself to this new season, you *must* master greed; you *must* put God first in your life! God wants to bless you, but He cannot give you more while you are still carrying around the little green monster of greed. You may also need a change of attitude about your job so you begin to see it as your calling. Some will need to stop being secret agents and become bold ambassadors for Christ in their workplaces. Others will need to make a new commitment to be faithful and godly stewards over the wealth they have or the assets they manage for others.

God is shaking everything that can be shaken in this season so that His *unshakable* Kingdom can surface. The Kingdom of God is about to flood the business mountain with a tsunami of creative ideas, knowledge, and wisdom, and you can have a part in it. In the past, we have not always used the resources we have for God in the mountain of business, but those days are over. God wants to share His wealth of wisdom with us to make us successful in this mountain. We are breaking out of Egypt and breaking Egypt out of us. Christians who are on a mission for God are about to become overwhelmingly successful in the mountain of business!

In the next chapter, we talk about the mountain of government. God expects every Christian to be engaged in government, and for some, this is their mountain. God says in Romans 13:1: *"Be a good citizen. All governments are under God. Insofar as there is peace and order, it's God's order. So live responsibly as a citizen"* (MSG). But what are God's expectations when the mountain of government becomes unjust and abusive and promotes wickedness?

CHAPTER SEVEN

The Government Mountain

We who live in America should thank God for the privilege to be citizens of the greatest nation the world has ever seen. Regardless of its shortcomings, I believe it is by far the best and most liberating place to live. If you have traveled overseas, you have seen firsthand "there is no place like home"—the United States of America. Yet, great as it is, our government desperately needs the influence of the Kingdom of God. Our mountain of government needs an influx of *real* Christians into its hills, summits, and peaks.

God has a strategic plan to bring righteousness to our government. So, let me remind you that God's Son did not come to earth on vacation. Jesus did not suffer and die to build churches on street corners. He came as part of God's strategic plan to restore humanity, the earth, and every living thing in it to Himself. Although He could have used other means to carry out His purpose, He chose us, the Body of Christ, to restore His Kingdom to every nation through the mountains of society, including the mountain of government.

There's a day coming when the mountain of God's House will be The Mountain—solid, towering over all mountains. All nations will

*river toward it, people from all over set out for it. They'll say, "**Come,
let's climb God's Mountain,** go to the House of the God of Jacob.
**He'll show us the way He works so we can live the way we're
made…** "* (Isaiah 2:2-3 MSG).

In times past, many have thought this Scripture meant that Christians
should leave the mountains of society and isolate themselves in church culture. However, God was declaring that the Church ("the house of God") is
to be a training ground, a place where people will go to learn how to live
effectively, use their gifts successfully, and satisfy the purpose for which they
were created in the mountains of their calling.

Nations Under God

The concept of government, as opposed to anarchy, is from God. His
Kingdom is organized, not chaotic, and is a model for the governments of
humankind. Even satan, the enemy of man, is organized with "principalities,
powers, and rulers in high places" (see Eph. 6:12). Scripture makes clear that
"there is no authority except from God." Romans 13:1-2, 5-6 says:

> *Let **every** person **be loyally subject to the governing (civil)
> authorities**. For there is **no authority except from God** [by
> His permission, His sanction], and those that exist do so by God's
> appointment. Therefore he who resists and sets himself up against the
> authorities resists what God has appointed and arranged [in divine
> order]. And those who resist will bring down judgment upon themselves
> [receiving the penalty due them].… Therefore **one must be subject,
> not only to avoid God's wrath and escape punishment, but also
> as a matter of principle and for the sake of conscience**. For this
> same reason you pay taxes, for [the civil authorities] are official servants
> under God, devoting themselves to attending to this very service* (AMP).

This Scripture means that God has given to humankind the organiza-
tional philosophy of government and has released authority to the system

of government a nation chooses. However, it does not mean that God condones everyone in government, or that communism or any other repressive governmental system is from God, or that a demon-possessed ruler, such as Hitler, is God's gift to humankind.

Manner Over Mode

Proverbs 29:2 explains: *"When good people run things, everyone is glad, but when the ruler is bad, everyone groans"* (MSG). This means that the form of government is not as important as the righteous manner of the people who run it. A godly dictator could give his people a good government as long as he lived, even though dictatorship is not a good system of government: *"Righteousness exalts a nation, but sin is a reproach to any people"* (Prov. 14:34). Every mode of government, including democracy, is only as good as the principles its leaders use to govern.

The United States of America was founded predominantly by born-again Christians who sought to escape from governmental tyranny. They were looking for their "promised land," a place of religious, economic, and personal freedom. However, as a colony of the repressive monarchy of England, they and their children continued to be tyrannized. Eventually, they yearned to be free from their oppressor and desired to form their own government—a government that would represent their interests without limiting their freedom of choice.

Based on their understanding of the Bible, the founders created a new form of government, a system of governing unlike any that the earth had seen: a government with its powers equally distributed between its three branches—the judicial, the legislative, and the executive. This new method of governing was derived from the form of government found in the Kingdom of God as stated in Isaiah 33:22, *"For the* LORD *is our Judge* [judicial], *the* LORD *is our Lawgiver* [legislative], *the* LORD *is our King* [executive]; *He will save us."*

A Sampling of the Founding Fathers' Beliefs

The founders of the United States of America were men of deep religious convictions based on the Bible and in Jesus Christ. Of the 56 men who signed the Declaration of Independence, 24 (almost half) held seminary or Bible school degrees and were qualified for full-time ministry. The following quotes give an overview of their strong moral and spiritual convictions, which greatly affected the founding of the United States and the creation of its government:

- *George Washington—First U.S. President*—"To the distinguished character of Patriot, it should be our highest glory to add the more distinguished character of Christian."[1]

- *John Adams—Second U.S. President and Signer of the Declaration of Independence*—"I will avow that I then believed, and now believe, that those general principles of Christianity are as eternal and immutable as the existence and attributes of God."[2]

- *Thomas Jefferson—Third U.S. President, Drafter and Signer of the Declaration of Independence*—"I am a real Christian—that is to say, a disciple of the doctrines of Jesus Christ."[3]

- *John Hancock—First Signer of the Declaration of Independence*—"Continue steadfast and, with a proper sense of your dependence on God, nobly defend those rights which heaven gave, and no man ought to take from us."[4]

- *Benjamin Franklin—Signer of the Declaration of Independence and the U.S. Constitution*—"Here is my Creed. I believe in one God, the Creator of the Universe. That He governs it by His Providence. That He ought to be worshiped."[5]

- *Samuel Adams—Signer of the Declaration of Independence and Father of the American Revolution*—"…We cannot better express ourselves than by humbly supplicating the Supreme Ruler of the world that the rod of tyrants may be broken to pieces, and the oppressed made free again; …by promoting and speedily bringing on that holy and happy period when the kingdom of our Lord and Saviour Jesus Christ may be everywhere established, and all people everywhere willingly bow to the sceptre of Him who is Prince of Peace."[6]

- *James Madison—Fourth U.S. President*—"Cursed be all that learning that is contrary to the cross of Christ."[7]

- *James Monroe—Fifth U.S. President*—"Let us then, unite in offering our most grateful acknowledgments for these blessings to the Divine Author of All Good."[8]

- *John Quincy Adams—Sixth U.S. President*—"Whoever believes in the divine inspiration of the Holy Scriptures must hope that the religion of Jesus shall prevail throughout the earth. …till the Lord shall have made 'bare His holy arm in the eyes of all the nations, and all the ends of the earth shall see the salvation of our God' (Isa. 52:10)."[9]

- *William Penn—Founder of Pennsylvania*—"I do declare to the whole world that we believe the Scriptures to contain a declaration of the mind and will of God…. We accept them as the words of God Himself."[10]

- *Alexander Hamilton—Signer of the Declaration of Independence and Ratifier of the U.S. Constitution*—"I have carefully examined the evidences of the Christian religion, and if I was sitting as a juror upon its authenticity I would unhesitatingly give my verdict in its favor."[11]

- *Patrick Henry—Ratifier of the U.S. Constitution*—"It cannot be emphasized too strongly or too often that this great nation was founded, not by religionists, but by Christians; not on religions, but on the gospel of Jesus Christ. For this very reason peoples of other faiths have been afforded asylum, prosperity, and freedom of worship here."[12]

Failing of the Founders?

Yes, many of the founding fathers had issues. They were far from perfect, but in recent times more attention has been focused on their shortcomings than their strengths and incredible accomplishments. The tragedy of slavery, however, the greatest stain on America, was not dealt with when the states united to become a nation. Although many of the founders wanted to prohibit slavery, they compromised to achieve unity and left slavery a decision for each state, hoping to deal with it after the War for Independence was won. Our nation still suffers from the consequences of that decision. However, the founders loved God, and to the best of their knowledge and ability, they created a system of government on God's principles, and that sets the United States apart from every nation created before or since.

On the Brink of a Tipping Point

For decades, people who were called to the mountain of government sat in their churches frustrated. They were told the rapture was "just around the corner," so why waste time in politics when they could not make a difference anyway? However, when people from God's camp departed government, the vacuum was filled by those from the other camp.

Your Duties in Government

Everyone, especially Christians, is called to take part in government at some level. We should all keep ourselves knowledgeable about current affairs, know what our government is doing, know about bills being proposed and passed, be familiar with the people who presently hold positions of power locally and nationally, and know about those running for office. And we should vote for the people who best represent our Christian principles and beliefs regardless of party affiliation.

This is the time for Christians to speak up in the political forum and be heard about what they believe constitutes a good, godly, and righteous government. A government that does not suppress what the founders called our "inalienable rights." We should support with our efforts and finances people with godly principles who are running for office.

Third Great Awakening

If America is to have a "Third Great Awakening," a nationwide revival, it cannot come from the church mountain *alone*. If you study recent notable outpourings of the Holy Spirit, you will discover that many people were blessed for a season, but the outpourings created no lasting impact on their surrounding communities, states, or nations. While we have enjoyed the presence of God in our churches, some in government have laughed at us and felt free, without a godly influence, to make laws and decisions that advance an anti-Christian agenda.

The people at the pinnacle of the seven kingdoms of culture were put there by one power or another—God or satan. Because we have not desired powerful or influential positions, we have given them away, by default, to the other camp. Our negligence has actually ratified the establishment of ungodly forces in places of power. Consequently, to transform our nation, we *must* go outside the church to have an effect.

As our nation moved from an agrarian society to an industrial one, and now to the information age, the Church has not kept pace. Except for the use of electricity, many of our churches remain in the horse-and-buggy era. God never changes, but the Church must adjust to stay current and remain relevant to society. A "bunker mentality" is costing us our Christian culture, and the Church is reaching a tipping point when it could lose it ability to come back to a place of influence in our culture.

Look at the condition of the Church in Europe. Even in once-godly Christian nations, citadels of the Protestant Reformation, the Church has become irrelevant, and instead their societies have come under the influence of humanism and socialism. This is the direction in which powerful people of influence desire to lead our nation as well.

Some would say the Church of America has already lost its ability to make a difference. But there is still hope for our land because some in the Church are waking up to their gifts and calling to the mountains of society. The emergence of the seven-mountain strategy is so timely that we believe it is not too late! There is hope, and that hope rests squarely in the hands of those who are determined to fulfill their purpose and take the places of influence for which God has prepared them.

Ten Times Better Than Your Contemporaries?

You probably remember the story of Daniel and the "three Hebrew children," but did you know that an unrighteous king found them to be ten times better than their contemporaries? The Babylonian empire defeated the kingdom of Judah and took their best and brightest young Hebrew men back to Babylon to serve in the government. Among this group was Daniel and those who were renamed Shadrach, Meshach, and Abed-Nego. After three years of training, they were evaluated and brought before the king for a final vetting:

> *...**God gave them knowledge and skill in all literature and wisdom**; and Daniel had **understanding in all visions and dreams**.... Then the king interviewed them, and among them all none was found like Daniel, Hananiah, Mishael, and Azariah.... **And in all matters of wisdom and understanding about which the king examined them, he found them ten times better** than all the magicians and astrologers who were in all his realm...* (Daniel 1:17,19-20).

God gave those young men favor and ability, beyond their natural gifts, to grasp and understand wisdom. Because they were anointed for government and serving in their mountain, God made them ten times wiser than everyone else. A day came when Daniel not only interpreted the king's dream but also described his dream. In that moment, the mightiest man on the earth, King Nebuchadnezzar, learned there is a *real* God and Daniel received a significant promotion:

> *The king answered Daniel, and said, "Truly your God is the God of gods, the Lord of kings, and a revealer of secrets, since you could reveal this secret." Then the king promoted Daniel and gave him many great gifts; and he made him ruler over the whole province of Babylon, and chief administrator over all the wise men of Babylon (Daniel 2:47-48).*

Need a Boost?

God has all the answers you need in your mountain of influence, and His supernatural boost can make you smarter and more effective than your contemporaries.

The world is discovering, like King Nebuchadnezzar did, that its experts and wise men do not have the answers it needs. Mountains of influence will put godly men and women, who operate at a level ten times greater than their colleagues, on the fast-track to success. However, the opposite is also true:

> *You are the salt of the earth; but if the salt loses its flavor, how shall it be seasoned? It is then good for nothing but to be thrown out and trampled underfoot by men (Matthew 5:13).*

Christianity has nearly reached the point where it has nothing to offer society, and when the world decides the Church has no taste, "flavor," or value, they will throw it out as irrelevant. However, now is the time for Christian government leaders to arise. It is the moment for Christians who are honest and moral, those with the answers that no one else has, to come to places of power and influence, not only in government but in all the mountains of influence.

The Demonic Stronghold Over Government—Corruption

People who are not spiritually prepared for having power will succumb to the vices that power awakens in their unregenerated souls. God not only made Moses the leader of a nation but also gave him tremendous power: He could part oceans and speak things into existence, calling forth water from a rock. So God had to create in Moses a meek spirit. He probably acquired that spirit during the 40 years he lived as an outcast on the backside of the desert. Some who stumble through deserts today are being schooled in humility so they can become a Moses to their mountain of influence.

Scripture says, *"…Moses was very humble, more than all men who were on the face of the earth"* (Num. 12:3). God could entrust Moses with great power without being concerned that he would create his own kingdom and cause a church split. Those who would wield great power must never lose their humility or forget who raised them up.

Once during a service, I prophesied to a man that he would become the leader of his Latin American country. He was so humble that he knelt before me and begged for my blessing. God did a miracle: This man who had no chance of winning was elected when all the other candidates were disqualified by a scandal that was exposed before the election. Years later, a pastor friend invited me to go with him to this same country for a meeting. I asked God and He said, "Go." My only intention was to accompany my friend, not to minister there, but while we were en route, the Lord told me that I was to minister to the country's president.

110

So, it came as no surprise when my friend told me that we had an audience with the president. When we were escorted into his office, I barely recognized the arrogant and prideful man before me. He remembered me and made pleasant conversation with us until I told him that I had a Word for him from the Lord. God then used me to tell him that he would lose his office and be stripped of his power because of his arrogance. *"God sets Himself against the proud, but He shows favor to the humble"* (James 4:6 NLT).

In only a matter of weeks, this man was chased out of office and the country.

The Corrupting Influence of Power Makes Necessary:

- Distribution of power

- Accountability for those in power

- Integrity in those who are holders of power.

Psalm 89:14 says about the rule of the Kingdom of God, *"Righteousness and justice are the foundation of Your throne...."* *Righteousness* speaks of issues like abortion, but *justice* is different. Justice goes beyond having right laws and is about showing compassion and mercy upon those who deserve it, like the poor and needy. The responsibility of helping the poor should be a function of the Church, not government. One day, I believe, that responsibility will return to us.

Profiles in Courage

Shadrach, Meshach, and Abed-Nego had found favor in the Babylonian government, but then King Nebuchadnezzar had a giant gold statue of himself built and commanded everyone to bow to it. These three young men decided to take a stand of uncompromising righteousness and made it known that they would not bow.

The king was furious when he heard of their refusal to show obeisance to his image and decided to make an example of them. He had them bound and thrown into a fiery furnace that had been heated seven times hotter than normal, so hot that it killed some of the king's guards. There was some way of looking into the furnace, and as the king watched with anticipation, he was soon disappointed when nothing happened to the three except their bonds disappeared. Imagine the wonder and perhaps fear on the face of the king when he exclaimed, *"I see four men loose, walking in the midst of the fire; and they are not hurt, and the form of the fourth is like the Son of God"* (Dan. 3:25).

That fourth person was the God who is "a very present help in time of trouble" (see Ps. 46:1), Jesus, the Good Shepherd, who watches over His own and comes to us in our hour of need. The three Hebrew young men took a moral stand, and Christ stood with them. They came out of the furnace unharmed, without even the smell of smoke, and the same government that had persecuted them promoted them to high positions. God is not afraid of the challenge when His children face a morally corrupt government, and so we can have confidence to make the same stand. He may not keep us out of the heat, but He will most certainly walk us through it to victory.

Pounce or Pray?

A few years ago, God said to me, "I did not call you to be a political commentator," and I was reminded of the things I had said about a previous president. He went on to say, "I have called you to pray for your president and those in authority." When we see unrighteousness, injustice, and corruption in government, our *natural* response is to condemn it, but God has called His people to a *supernatural* response—we are to pray for them:

> *I urge you, first of all, to pray for all people. As you make your requests, plead for God's mercy upon them, and give thanks. Pray this way for*

kings and all others who are in authority, so that we can live in peace and quietness, in godliness and dignity. This is good and pleases God our Savior, for He wants everyone to be saved and to understand the truth (1 Timothy 2:1-4 NLT).

Before complaining and placing blame for how degenerate and evil things have become in our nation, we should look at the situation from God's point of view. To find the ultimate reason for the state of our nation and the world, we should consider who Jesus left in charge when He departed the planet. We are not responsible for what past generations left undone, but we will be held accountable for what we do *now*—now that we understand God's purpose for His people in general and for us in particular.

On a Practical Level

What good do Christians' criticisms accomplish in the mountain of government? But what *could we do* if the Church blessed instead of blasted? What might happen if, as an alternative to complaining, we did what God instructed—pray?

If My people who are called by My name will humble themselves, and pray and seek My face, and turn from their wicked ways, then I will hear from heaven, and will forgive their sin and heal their land (2 Chronicles 7:14).

With Christianity at a tipping point, it is time for each person in the Body of Christ to answer the question Jesus asked more than 2,000 years ago—"*. . . When the Son of Man comes, will He really find faith on the earth?*" (Luke 18:8). We cannot shrug this off; if it was not a serious question would Jesus have asked it?

Would you pledge to do your part by using your gifts and talents to fulfill your calling to be a godly influence in your mountain? God is not done with us! He is not finished with America, but each of us must do our part in the mountain of government and in the mountain of our individual calling.

Our next mountain is that of media. This mountain can be particularly intimidating, and for that reason the Church has often sought to create its own separate forms of media. But, as we will see, God is calling us to boldly infiltrate this kingdom with His good news.

Endnotes

1. *The Writings of Washington*, 342-43, quoted at http://christianity. about.com/od/independenceday/a/foundingfathers.htm (accessed April 2011).

2. From a letter dated June 28, 1813, to Thomas Jefferson, http:// christianity.about.com/od/independenceday/a/foundingfathers. htm.

3. *The Writings of Thomas Jefferson*, 385, http://christianity.about. com/od/independenceday/a/foundingfathers.htm.

4. *History of the United States of America, Vol. II*, 229, http:// christianity.about.com/od/independenceday/a/foundingfathers. htm.

5. From a letter to Ezra Stiles, president of Yale University, dated March 9, 1790, http://christianity.about.com/od/ independenceday/a/foundingfathers.htm.

6. Proclamation of a Day of Fast as governor of Massachusetts, March 20, 1797, http://christianity.about.com/od/ independenceday/a/foundingfathers_2.htm.

7. Mark A. Beliles and Stephen K. McDowell, *America's Providential History*, 93, http://christianity.about.com/od/independenceday/a/foundingfathers_2.htm.

8. Monroe made this statement in his second annual message to Congress on November 16, 1818, http://christianity.about.com/od/independenceday/a/foundingfathers_2.htm.

9. *Life of John Quincy Adams*, 248, http://christianity.about.com/od/independenceday/a/foundingfathers_2.htm.

10. *Treatise of the Religion of the Quakers*, 355, http://christianity.about.com/od/independenceday/a/foundingfathers_2.htm.

11. *Famous American Statesmen*, 126, http://christianity.about.com/od/independenceday/a/foundingfathers_3.htm.

12. M.E. Bradford, *The Trumpet Voice of Freedom: Patrick Henry of Virginia*, iii, http://christianity.about.com/od/independenceday/a/foundingfathers_3.htm.

CHAPTER EIGHT
Media—The Mind-Molder Mountain

Advertising executive William Bernbach said, "All of us who professionally use the mass media are the shapers of society. We can vulgarize that society. We can brutalize it. Or we can help lift it onto a higher level."[1] One of the greatest influences of society is media. To be effective in spreading the Good News, the Church must not only be adept at using the modern methods of communications, it must also infiltrate and influence the mountain of media. In our information age, the message that media conveys today becomes tomorrow's mindset.

We Have a Media Mandate

With the revelation that God wants His people to bring His influence into the cultures of nations through the seven-mountain strategy comes the mandate to put it into action. God never reveals a truth merely to give a new intellectual insight; He expects us to put new understandings into practice. Embedded within each revelation is the divine empowerment to carry it out. We perform our mission by living Christlike lives, by finding and entering our assigned mountain of influence, and by implementing the principles and power of God's Word and Kingdom in our mountain.

Communication Is Power

For the first time in our nation's history, teenagers make up the largest segment of the population. The church mountain has poured effort and resources into reaching teens, but the other mountains of influence are arrayed on the other side of this tug-of-war for their souls, and their principal means of influencing youth is media. In the information age, media is king, which means that our children are constantly bombarded with media messages based on a godless worldview. When the Church disengaged from media, it forfeited its opportunity to make use of the influence of the media realm. God, however, has spoken prophetically that He will "raise up a 'media army' in our day that will infiltrate this kingdom."

Paul said in Romans 1:16, *"For I am not ashamed of the **gospel** of Christ, for it **is the power of God** to salvation for everyone who believes...."* The Greek word translated *Gospel* is *evangelion,* which means "good news." Paul was pointing out that the Good News has power; however, all news has power. One has the power to free captives, and the other has power to take captive.

The prophet Isaiah declared:

> *How beautiful upon the mountains are the feet of him who brings good news, who proclaims peace, who brings glad tidings of good things, who proclaims salvation, who says to Zion, "Your God reigns!"* (Isaiah 52:7)

Although this Scripture applies to everyone who takes the Good News of God's Kingdom into one of the mountains of culture, it seems especially appropriate for those in the media mountain. Those who bring news, proclaim peace, bring glad tiding of good things, and proclaim salvation are the ones with "beautiful feet" (feet in Scripture can refer to the values that guide our steps). This Scripture is saying that when you are guided by godly ideals, find your mountain, and become a media voice for God, you have authority there to declare the power of God's Kingdom with such influence that it reshapes culture, drives out oppression, and creates enlightenment that can transform lives.

Farming for Souls

The purpose for entering and influencing the mountains of culture is to bring those who are within those mountains and those influenced by them to "call upon Jesus." If you are wondering how that is accomplished, Paul explains it in Romans 10:14-15,17:

How then shall they call on Him in whom they have not believed? And how shall they believe in Him of whom they have not heard? And how shall they hear without a preacher? And how shall they preach unless they are sent? ...So then faith comes by hearing, and hearing by the word of God.

The Cycle of Kingdom Harvest

1. *Send*—Someone must go;

2. *Preach*—To communicate the Good News;

3. *Hear*—Expressing it in ways hearers can understand;

4. *Believe*—Hearers can then accept the truth and;

5. *Call*—Ask Jesus to forgive and transform their lives.

The Church is in the media or communications business, and the higher the quality of the message, the better the results. That does not mean we dilute the message to make it more pleasant. It does mean we should give up our King James verbiage, religious ways, and traditional methods to embrace new ways of expressing spiritual truths in which everyone can relate.

Two-Edged Sword of Media

The ways information comes to people are constantly changing, and the Church has to at least keep up; but better yet, it should become a leader in the evolution of communication. Knowledgeable people tell us that cell phones, as well as being personal communication devices, will one day take the place of computers and become media centers for music and television. Consequently, merely having a couple of Christian television networks is not nearly enough—and actually never has been. We have to be engaged with Facebook, MySpace, Twitter, and other social networking sites, in addition to the older methods of communication: radio and television. We must take advantage of every means to convey our message, in addition to sending people to the media mountain as ambassadors for the Kingdom of God.

The mountain of media has become a tool in satan's hands to attack and denigrate the Church and its message. Yet, we have the promise that:

> *"No weapon formed against you shall prosper, and every tongue which rises against you in judgment you shall condemn. This is the heritage of the servants of the LORD, and their righteousness is from Me," says the LORD* (Isaiah 54:17).

The media weapon that the enemy has used so effectively against the Church is not evil in itself. It is like a two-edged sword that may be used to carve up what is good or chop down evil and create an opening for God's Kingdom. It is time for media to be turned for good, and we know that is possible because *"...God causes all things to work together for good to those who love God, to those who are called according to His purpose"* (Rom. 8:28 NASB).

Fear Is the Demonic Sword Holding Sway Over Media

God is raising up a new breed of uncompromisingly righteous, fearlessly courageous, and bold-as-a-lion media warriors—people who will seize Goliath's sword!

Media knows that the more fearful its message, the more people are drawn to it. Consequently, it looks for the negative to report and hungrily pursues a negative slant on every subject, especially things relating to Christians and the Church. The media has the power to threaten and even destroy people. Because of the media bias against all things Christian, believers need to be ready to stand up to the media's abuse of its power and be willing to risk their reputations to do what is right and righteous. The church must be uncompromisingly righteous plus outrageously fearless and declare to the monster of media, "I'm not afraid of you." Solomon said, *"The wicked flee when no one pursues, but **the righteous are bold as a lion**"* (Prov. 28:1).

You may remember the Old Testament story of Elijah turning a nation back to God found in First Kings 19. He called down fire upon a wet sacrifice, executed 450 prophets of Baal, ended a drought, and outran the king's chariot. But the next day, Jezebel, King Ahab's wicked wife, sent a messenger (her media device) to Elijah with a communiqué. She threatened to end the prophet's life in the same way he had slaughtered her prophets. Her message was so effective that when Jezebel's curse was *spoken* the Bible says that Elijah *saw* her message.

With fresh memories of the bloody carnage of Baal's prophets, the message imprinted on Elijah's mind to such a degree that he visualized himself being executed. He became so overwhelmed with fear that he ran for his life to the neighboring country of Judah. There he left his servant and fled into the desert to die:

> ...*He came to a lone broom bush and collapsed in its shade, wanting in the worst way to be done with it all—to just die: "Enough of this, GOD! Take my life..."* (1 Kings 19:4 MSG).

The things Elijah experienced—isolating himself, becoming abnormally despondent and depressed, experiencing an unusual physical fatigue or exhaustion—are all signs of spiritual warfare. Jezebel did not *do* anything, she only *said* things, and yet the man of God was ready to lie down and die. There is a tremendous power in words, and media wields that power and uses it either for good or evil. As you may recall, God strengthened and encouraged Elijah. Then he decided to rejoin the living and soon afterward found his successor, Elisha.

Seizing Goliath's Sword

The well-known story of David and Goliath contains Kingdom keys for those who would scale the mountain of media. You will recall that, *"The Philistines stood on a mountain on one side, and Israel stood on a mountain on the other side, with a valley between them"* (1 Sam. 17:3). Symbolically, the church mountain was standing opposed to one of the other mountains.

Meanings of Names and Words to Help Understand This Key

- *Philistine* means "wander in routine dust" (lost in the confusion of carnality).

- *Goliath* means "to capture, strip and shame, then exile" (media wants to take people's territory, strip them of their reputation, and exile them to a place of ineffectiveness).

- *Dismayed* means "to break down by violence, confusion, fear, or despair; to be crushed, discouraged, and demoralized."

- *Afraid* means "the emotional and intellectual anticipation of harm or to fear."

Twice a day Goliath bellowed his challenge for Israel to send someone to fight with him. The result was *they were **dismayed** and greatly **afraid**"* (1 Sam. 17:11). To dismay or demoralize and to make afraid or cause the anticipation of harm is the portrait of abuse. Goliath was ruling Israel's army not by his sword but by his words. It is easy to think we would have behaved differently, but having witnessed it firsthand, I can tell you it is amazing what good people will do when threatened with public disgrace. This is a strategy of satan, and God wants His Church to understand satan's tactics. As the Latin proverb says, "Forewarned is forearmed."

The Church Mountain Versus the Media Mountain

The Church has misunderstood the purpose of media and its importance to spreading the Good News, and we have created our own media for our own audience. There is a subculture of media called Christian television, Christian radio, Christian movies, and Christian novels. All this is great for Christians, but it fails to make use of this powerful sword to penetrate society. As a result, Christianity does not have power in media's true places of influence. However, the Church is beginning to understand that we have an obligation to bring righteousness to the mountain of media. It is time to turn around a media that has lost all objectivity, become an advocate of homosexual and immoral lifestyles and the theory of evolution, and has set itself as the enemy of everything Christian.

Goliath was preaching to Israel day and night his message of fear and doom, and they were not countering his message. Much like today's Church, they had no media, no voice. We do not know what to do when media comes against us and often run away when we should attack. In my season of warfare with the media, everything the lawyers told me to do was contrary to what the Bible says. Not knowing what to do, I listened when they told me not to defend myself and not to say anything, and that was the wrong course.

Dagger of Depravity

Our major television networks fill their programming with horoscopes, yoga, sorcery, mediums, talking to the dead, and other New Age practices. They are trying to pierce our culture to make things seem normal that are not normal but devilish. The immoral viewpoint our children are exposed to by media is appalling, and it can be found in almost everything they watch. *Are you aware that 95 percent of all teenagers have seen pornography on the Internet?* We are unable to shield our precious children from the onslaught of evil in the media. The answer for Christians is not to run away, hide in monasteries, and destroy our televisions and computers but to go on the attack to take back all the summits of media.

Once prepared for his battle, David stepped onto the battlefield, and the giant Goliath cursed him by his gods. David, however, did not ignore the cursing but answered forcefully:

> *…You come to me with a sword, with a spear, and with a javelin. But I come to you in the name of the LORD of hosts, the God of the armies of Israel, whom you have defied* (1 Samuel 17:45).

David told Goliath that this battle was not about the two of them but a fight between the Philistines and God's people, so it was God's battle. If we can connect with the understanding that God is after the mountains of society—He wants the mountains of family, education, government, entertainment, business, *and media*—we will have the courage David showed when facing his giant. God is looking for Davids, for warriors He can dispatch to represent His interests who will take back what is rightfully His.

When Jesus was tempted by satan, he could legitimately say that all the kingdoms of this world belonged to him, but no more. Jesus defeated the devil and took back the keys of authority and dominion satan had fleeced from Adam. The day is coming when *"…the kingdoms of this world have become the kingdoms of our Lord and of His Christ, and He shall reign forever and ever!"* (Rev. 11:15).

You know the rest of the story. David hurled a stone, and Goliath fell. David prevailed over the Philistine giant with a sling and stone and killed him, but David did not have a sword, so he took the enemy's sword (symbolic of media) and cut off the giant's head. The sword (media) was not evil but only used for evil. Those who would topple the evil media giant need only a "smooth" or well-crafted "stone" or device and the courage to use it with a David-like "knowing" that God will make it sufficient for its purpose. Those with a media mandate who will dare step onto the media battlefield will gain possession of media's mighty sword.

Goliath's sword had killed thousands of people in battle. It had made widows and orphans, slain the innocent, and corrupted a generation. But the moment David touched that sword, it became God's sword. When the Church retakes the sword of Goliath, media, God will allow us to dispose of ruling powers. Then, instead of that sword carving out a humanistic or demonic agenda that divides and destroys, it will be used to open society to righteousness and Kingdom truths. That does not mean we will not have news, movies, novels, etc.; it means that those things will be influenced by God's Kingdom.

For 100 years, the media has promoted evil as good, made criminals heroes, ridiculed government and authority, and vilified Christianity. Is it not time for Christians who are called to the mountain of media to take back that sword?

Next, we talk about media's sister mountain, the mountain of arts and entertainment. At the time of the Renaissance, the world burst forth with a new level of artistic achievement. Today, we are entering another renaissance in the mountain of arts and entertainment. In the next chapter, you will learn that art is not only going to become greater, but new, never-before-seen expressions of art will be developed.

Endnote

1. http://thinkexist.com/quotation/all_of_us_who_professionally_use_the_mass_media/226984.html (accessed April 2011).

CHAPTER NINE

The Mountain of Arts and Entertainment

More than 2,000 years ago, Jesus was speaking of our day when He said:

> *This **gospel of the kingdom** will be preached in all the world as a witness **to all the nations**, and **then the end will come*** (Matthew 24:14).

This Scripture tells us that in the last days, the "Gospel of the Kingdom" will be made known to all nations. It infers that this broadcast of the Gospel will be so powerful (through the seven mountains of influence) that all the nations of earth will come to understand the truth about God's Kingdom. At that point, the mission of the Church will be accomplished, and the end will come. Today is that day; this is the season when some in the Church are rediscovering their Christ-intended purpose to take the *Kingdom* Gospel into this world's kingdoms of culture. How about you? Could the mountain of arts and entertainment be your destination? Is it possible that you have a hidden gift or need to rediscover a forgotten dream?

Mountain Missionaries

For decades, and even millennia, the Church has preached a different Gospel from the one Jesus preached. Although the truth of salvation is vitally important as the foundation of the Gospel of the Kingdom and the most important chapter in God's love story for humankind, it is not the full story. God coauthored the chapter of salvation with Christ, but in His next chapter, titled "The Kingdoms of Earth Become the Kingdoms of Our Lord" (see Rev. 11:15), God wants to coauthor with you and me.

This is the day when the supernatural and miraculous, the works that Jesus did and "greater works" (see John 14:12), will move outside the Church to be performed by ordinary people in the seven mountains of culture. Signs and wonders will be a witness and validation of the supremacy of the Kingdom of God to every nation of the earth. This is the day for multitudes of mountain missionaries to be brought forth—people whose lives are so blessed, so anointed, and so powerful that their presence and their works will impact and change their mountains. Through them the world will discover that the Kingdom of God is an incredibly wonderful place and many people will look for how they can get to God's Kingdom.

Who Wants to Take Part?

QUESTION: Who do you suppose God is calling to be mighty mountain missionaries: Those who already have great ministries? Those who pastor megachurches? Those who hold large salvation and healing crusades around the world?

ANSWER: No! They have their place in the scheme of things, but God is looking for common, ordinary people who "get it"—those who understand what God is doing in this season and want to take part.

QUESTION: Do you believe the seven-mountain strategy is God's plan for this age? Do you want to be one of God's mighty mountain men or women? Are you willing to be healed and cleansed of things that keep you from being and becoming the person God created you to be?

ANSWER: If you said yes to the above, you got the job. You're hired! You're *the* man (or woman)!

A Second Renaissance

About A.D. 1500, Martin Luther, a German priest and university professor of theology, had a divine insight and wrote a paper called "The 95 Theses," which he nailed to the door of the All Saints Church (their university bulletin board). He stated that the only way to salvation was by grace, and the only approach to grace was by faith—solely grace and only faith. About that same time others had similar spiritual insights and the truth of salvation by faith began penetrating a world clouded for almost 1,000 years by darkness. Previously the Church had taught that people could receive salvation by doing certain things: through penance, pain, keeping traditions, and other religious activities. The restoration of this most basic spiritual truth caused the Protestant Reformation.

The Protestant Reformation just *happened* to coincide with the Renaissance. What a curious coincidence. Was it just a twist of fate, or did one thing have to do with the other? Historians cannot agree on the actual cause of the Renaissance. As humanists, most have never considered the explanation Christians find most likely: When the heavens opened with the truth of salvation by grace, they remained open to release new scientific discoveries and artistic creativity into the minds of men. We are still experiencing the benefits of that exciting season.

With the recent rediscovery of the "Gospel of the Kingdom" message, another renaissance is about to occur. Like the former renaissance, it will not only impact the church mountain but will also revolutionize science, arts and entertainment, and all the other mountains of culture.

A Renaissance "Word"

I believe the Lord is saying that in this new renaissance season, there will be new expressions of music and art and new scientific break-throughs. When believers open the heavens by declaring new revelation, unbelievers benefit too. So "new things" will come from both Christians and non-Christians, just as they did in the first renaissance.

Only One Dream Away

Jacob was "in process" by God when he left home, fleeing his brother Esau, and headed to Padan Aram to visit Uncle Laban (see Gen. 28). No doubt you recall that Jacob had incurred Esau's wrath by impersonating him to Isaac and swindling Esau out of the blessing of the firstborn. One night during his journey, Jacob rested at a place call *Luz*, which means "a bent or crooked place." That evening Jacob dreamed of a ladder reaching to Heaven where angels ascended and descended, and at the top of the ladder was the Lord. God spoke to Jacob and gave him the same blessing He had given to Abraham and Isaac, and then went on to pledge:

> *Behold, I am with you and will keep you wherever you go, and will bring you back to this land; for I will not leave you until I have done what I have spoken to you* (Genesis 28:15).

The next morning when Jacob awoke, he was still in awe of his dream experience. So, he took the rock he had used for a pillow, set it up as a pillar, poured oil over it, and renamed that place *Bethel,* which means "house (habitation) of God." The day before Jacob's dream, the future looked bleak and he was full of fear. Jacob believed that his brother could be chasing him with the intention of killing him. He was fleeing to an unfamiliar place where he was expected to find a wife among relatives he did not know.

After his dream, everything changed for Jacob. Fear and dread about the future were gone, and he was filled with confidence and hope. His dream sustained him through the difficult days and years of process ahead, as he found his wife(s), served her deceitful father, and created a fortune in spite of his father-in-law. Nothing had changed in the natural realm, yet, because of his dream, everything had changed. God wants to do the same for you.

A Renaissance Key

When a revelation comes to anyone, anywhere, there is power in that revelation to transform his or her life and to renovate the mountain of influence to which the revelation refers. Every time you receive a prophetic promise that is awakened by revelation, two things happen:

1. *Revelation causes you to have ownership of the promise.* God only gives you an insight through Scripture, a vision, or a dream for things He wants you to have or do. Revelation creates faith, and faith is ownership because it contains a piece or "substance" of the future for which you hope (see Heb. 11:1).

2. *Revelation creates a new anointing.* This fresh bequest of power is meant to help you to fulfill your revelation.

That means when you receive a revelation about your mountain and get a fresh insight about your future, faith is born out of your new prophetic understanding. A promise is deposited in you that will change you and the landscape of your life regardless how Luz-like, crooked, and bent your life may seem at that moment.

You are only one dream, one revelation away from transformation—things being completely changed. You view your life in the natural and make decisions based on how you think things are. However, a new revelation gives you a *new view* that causes you to see things as God does. So, when Jacob awoke from his dream, he had a new revelation.

Revelation is a new knowing. Your knowing determines your doing, and your doing determines your outcomes. But first you need to rename your situation. It can no longer be called "twisted and bent" (Luz). You have to say of your circumstances "God resides (Bethel) in my situation." Revelation—when you act upon it—rewrites your future and gives you a reformation—yes, you could even call it a renaissance.

Sight and Sound Generation

We who are living in this amazing time are part of the "sight and sound" generation. Perhaps you have heard of *The Five Love Languages*, a book that teaches the various languages people use to communicate and experience love. Generations also have languages, and the present generation communicates and is communicated with through artistic creative expressions that make use of sights and sounds. That means to convey the Good News of the Kingdom of God to them, we have to show them Christ through demonstrations of the arts. And that is a big reason why it is vitally important for the Kingdom of God to invade the mountain of arts and entertainment.

Acts 8 tells the story of Phillip, who was just a regular guy who took the Gospel of the Kingdom of God to Samaria. This ordinary person preached Christ to overflow crowds at Samaria. He cast out devils and performed great miracles, and the Bible tells us, *"There was great joy in that city"* (Acts 8:8). This is what it looks like when a mountain kingdom of culture discovers the Gospel of the Kingdom of God.

However, if you go back in time before Phillip arrived in Samaria, things were very different. The city was under the influence of satan, captivated by a guy who "claimed to be someone great" (see Acts 8:9), the man called Simon the Sorcerer. Simon enthralled the city with his magic. However, Simon's influence abruptly ended when Phillip came preaching "...*the kingdom of God* and **the name of Jesus Christ**..." (Acts 8:12).

- *Samaria* represents the mountain of arts and entertainment that is enthralled with Simon-like people whom the enemy has positioned in places of power and influence.

- *Simon* represents the present-day mountain of arts and entertainment that has been taken from righteousness into unrighteousness and used as a means to control people. Witchcraft is manipulation, and Simon was operating in witchcraft and divination to influence his mountain.

- *Phillip* represents what happens when someone from the Kingdom of God (a more powerful kingdom) invades and proves the superiority of God's Kingdom by God-inspired works, which set the minds of people free from the works of the enemy.

Don't get the wrong idea; this has nothing to with holding tent meetings in Hollywood. Rather, it is about people called to the arts displaying to the world the creative and artistic power of God's Kingdom in the mountain of arts and entertainment.

A Scripture for Arts and Entertainment

*Behold, the former things have come to pass, and **new things I declare**.... Sing to the LORD **a new song,** and His praise from the ends of the earth...* (Isaiah 42:9-10).

God is saying that He is doing a "new thing" in this season, and He will tell His people about it before it happens. God is love, but He is also Creator, and waves of creativity emanate from Him whenever He manifests Himself. God's new things will cause us to sing a new song and display new and never-before-seen kinds of art. The minds of Christians in this mountain will have new thoughts; their souls will have new emotions; their words will have new expression; and their hands will have new creative powers. Behind this new wave of creativity, a surge of God's glory will spread to the "ends of the earth."

Ark of Inspiration

Once, while spending time with the Lord, I asked Him what it meant to sing Him a new song. He told me that singing an old song to Him was like getting a Hallmark card—nice but a little impersonal. A new song, however, one that bubbles up from the depths of the soul, makes Him feel intimately loved. God wants us to be like Him, and He is creative. David said, *"Sing a new song to him; play well and joyfully"* (Ps. 33:3 NCV).

Immediately after becoming king, David brought the Ark of Covenant to Jerusalem because he wanted to be close to the presence of God (see 2 Sam. 6). Before Jesus' sacrifice for the sins of mankind, God could not put His presence and glory *in* a person as He does today but only *on* them as an anointing. Yet, being in the presence of God was so important to David that he not only brought the Ark to Jerusalem but also created a new and more intensely personal form of worship.

The old form of worship had a priest go into the Holy of Holies, where the Ark rested, once a year with a sacrifice for the sins of Israel. But David took a different approach, and God allowed it. David placed an orchestra and choir in a tent with the Ark, and their sole job was to praise God 24 hours a day, 7 days a week. The psalms were not contrived by a group of talented songwriters; they were the artistic expressions of David and others who entered the tent and were touched by God's presence. Picture David walking into that tent filled with God's presence and not being able to contain himself and shouting, *"Bless the LORD, O my soul; and all that is within me, bless His holy name!"* (Ps. 103:1). Across the tent, David positioned a scribe whose job was to write down what had been revealed when the Holy Spirit of God touched the imaginations of men. One result was that David invented at least 25 musical instruments.

Your Unfinished Symphony

Do you have a lifelong regret that you did not finish your piano lessons or never took the time to learn how to play a guitar or some other musical instrument? Have you always wanted to do something in the arts—paint, create sculpture, dance, write music, or perform drama? *Any desire that lives past years of delay is a God-desire.* Some reading these words are going to write plays, movie scripts, and music, and create and invent new sights and sounds. It does not matter if the music you write is country and western or rap—all artistic gifts are given by God. Although some people use their gifts in ungodly ways, still their gifts are from God. Satan has nothing creative to give and can only influence what God has given.

It's never too late to release your gift!

Stronghold Over Arts and Entertainment—Immorality

Because the creative gift contains passion, creative people tend to be more susceptible to satan's corruption of *sexual* passion—immorality. Consequently, those who are gifted in the arts must first win the battle of immorality before reporting to their mountain for duty.

Immorality Is Overcome Through ...

1. *The Lordship of Christ*—Our lives need to be completely surrendered to Him in every area.

2. *Biblical truth*—Filling our hearts and minds with God's Word strengthens us against temptation.

3. *The empowering presence of the Holy Spirit*—Quality time in prayer fills our lives with great power.

*God wants you to be holy, so **you should keep clear of all sexual sin**. Then each of you will control your body and **live in holiness and honor—not in lustful passion** as the pagans do, in their ignorance of God and His ways* (1 Thessalonians 4:3-5 NLT).

Speaking of Sex

Although our culture tries to downplay sexual sin, it is one of the most damaging forms of sin because it affects the whole being: spirit, soul, and body. God created sex to be the uniting force of marriage and made it to cause "oneness"; it connects people at all three levels of their being. Outside of marriage, sex creates an inappropriate union that results in many harmful consequences. The Message version of the Bible says it plainly in its paraphrase of First Corinthians 6:14-16:

*God honored the Master's body by raising it from the grave. He'll treat yours with the same resurrection power. Until that time, remember that your bodies are created with the same dignity as the Master's body. You wouldn't take the Master's body off to a whorehouse, would you? I should hope not. **There's more to sex than mere skin on skin.***

Sex is as much spiritual mystery as physical fact. *As written in Scripture, "The two become one."*

Sex is a spiritual union—so, *morality matters!* It is never too late to become moral and clean up your life sexually. God wants you to live a life that is free of the great burdens this sin creates.

To overcome immorality, many people must also deal with a generational weakness of sexual lust. We have already talked about Gideon and how God required that he tear down his daddy's altars to Baal (his generational sins) before he could be successful in his calling to the mountain of government. What I did not mention before is that sexual immorality was a significant part of the worship of Baal; consequently, there was a spirit of immorality ruling over Gideon's family that needed to be torn down before he could take his place in his mountain. Like Gideon,

if you want to go beyond what your family *could not do,* then you have to do what they *would not do*—overcome generational curses of sexual lust.

Consider Samson, the Incredible Hulk of the Old Testament (see Judg. 14–16). He single-handedly killed thousands of the enemy and did not need a sword or spear but used whatever was at hand. One day he grabbed the jawbone of a donkey and defeated 1,000 men. No man could defeat him, but immorality brought him to his knees. Immorality is not something a person can play with and expect to escape from unscathed. Delilah was not Samson's temptation, she was his assassin, and immorality is the assassin crafted by satan to keep those of this mountain from their destiny. The lack of victory in only one area, sex, can keep you from living up to your potential.

If you believe the mountain of arts and entertainment may be your calling, I want to pray for you:

Father, I pray that in this moment You will begin a spiritual download of new thoughts, understanding, wisdom, and creativity to everyone reading these words. I pray for those who have been locked in a funk, unable to break free to express their creativity. I ask for something to awaken in them—new poetry, new novels, new songs, a new realm of expression and insight. Help them to break down old barriers and go to new places. Let Your new renaissance awaken the hearts of Your people. I pray also for those who have a longing to do something in the arts but have never done it. Help them to go back and find their gifts—stir it up, fan its flame, and build it up. Help them to reclaim its promise and potential. Lord, let the world see what the Kingdom of God can bring to arts and entertainment so that they may come to know You, the Author and Giver of every good thing. In Jesus' name I pray. Amen

In the next chapter, we venture into the kingdom of education. Everyone is affected by this kingdom and can have an influence upon it.

CHAPTER TEN
Paradigm Point—
The Mountain of Education

Paradigm means "a set of assumptions, concepts, values, and practices that amount to a way of viewing reality." What paradigm of reality or what worldview of the physical and spiritual worlds is the mountain of education teaching our children, grandchildren, and the youth of this nation? Is it:

- *Humanism*—The material universe is all that is real; there is no soul or spirit. Everything can be explained on the basis of natural law, including humans, who are considered a product of evolution. The only truth is what has been scientifically proven, only what can be observed by the five senses. No universal values or morals exist, only individual preferences or socially useful behavior, which is subject to change.

- *Theism*—An infinite, personal God exists who created a finite, material world. Reality is both material and spiritual. Humankind was uniquely created by God "in the image of God," which means that we are personal, eternal, spiritual, and biological. Truth about God is known through revelation, and His existence is attested to by creation. Truth about the material world is gained by revelation and the five senses in conjunction with rational thought. Moral values are not based on personal opinion but are absolute and have been expressed by God.

Most Christian children are taught from a humanistic point of view every school day and only hear a theistic standpoint a few hours a week at church and occasionally at home. Consequently, it should be no surprise when as many as 65 percent fall away from their Christian roots once they leave the influence of their parents. However, the understanding that God has a great future and an important purpose for their lives as an ambassador to a mountain of culture is the "missing piece" that makes Christianity relevant and exciting to young people—and in fact, to everyone.

When the Kingdom Comes Near

The Kingdom of God is not a religion or a euphemism for Heaven. It is a realm, a relationship, and a rule; it is *real*. Everyone has heard the expression "actions speak louder than words." Those on assignment to the kingdoms of culture "preach" God's Kingdom with their presence, their actions, and sometimes even with their words. They are preaching and impacting their mountain by merely taking the fruit of the Spirit and gifts of the Spirit to their coworkers as they respond to opportunities to love, heal, show mercy, raise the dead, share joy, and deliver from bondages. When asked where the power comes from to meet their own needs and the needs of those they touch, they can say as Jesus did, *"...The kingdom of God has come near to you"* (Luke 10:9). The Kingdom of God intersects humankind at its place of need, and it has the answers for all the needs of humankind.

What You Need to Know About Education

Education is not bad. Being educated is a good thing, but the quality of the education a person receives is determined by the who, what, and why of it:

- Who are the educators? Do they believe in a Christian worldview?

- What do they teach? Do they educate from a distorted understanding?

- Why are they teaching? Are they merely promoting an anti-God perspective?

God does not hold the state or federal government accountable for how our children are educated; He considers the family to have the first place of responsibility and then the church:

> [You] *train up a child in the way he should go [and in keeping with his individual gift or bent], and when he is old he will not depart from it* (Proverbs 22:6 AMP).

A Jewish rabbi told me that this Scripture alludes to a common practice of Jewish midwives. To encourage a newborn to take milk from the mother, the midwife will put olive oil or honey on the child's finger and have him taste it. When you give your children a taste of the real things of God—not religion but a life-empowering, Christ-honoring spirit—no matter how far away they might go, they will always remember the taste of honey, the sweet taste of the Kingdom of Heaven on their lips.

God feels strongly about how we raise our children. He even mentions it as one of the qualifications Abraham had to become the founder of the nation of Israel:

> *For I know him, that **he will command his children and his household after him, and they shall keep the way of the** LORD, to do justice and judgment; that the LORD may bring upon Abraham that which he hath spoken of him* (Genesis 18:19 KJV).

Balancing Punishment and Permissiveness

God not only expects fathers to train children in the right things, but He also expects fathers to train their children in the right way. *"Fathers, don't exasperate your children by coming down hard on them. Take them by the hand and lead them in the way of the Master"* (Eph. 6:4 MSG). This caution by God does not contradict the advice of Solomon about "sparing the rod and spoiling the child" (see Prov. 13:24) but completes it by removing heavy-handedness and rage from discipline. After all, God does not bloody our noses to convince us to be born again. Rather, *"...the goodness of God leads you to repentance"* (Rom. 2:4). God expects fathers to lead in love, not push out of anger.

Education Is Often Re-Education

Whether you have been to college or not, everyone has been to the University of Hard Knocks. I have a couple of PhDs. One is attested to by a paper hanging on my office wall. The other degree is verified by the stripes on my back. I'm sure you have them too. They confirm that you have made it through both good times and bad.

Most of what we have learned, we discovered while just living our lives. We pick up much of what we believe through our families, our culture, and our church experience or the lack of it. All of life teaches us things. Some of what we learn is true and good, and some is false and bad. When we come to the Kingdom, half (or more) of our learning is actually un-learning. God wants to replace the lies we have believed and teach us the truth. Paul said it like this:

> *So here's what I want you to do, God helping you: Take your everyday, ordinary life—your sleeping, eating, going-to-work, and walking-around life—and place it before God as an offering. Embracing what God does for you is the best thing you can do for Him. Don't become so well-adjusted to your culture that you fit into it without even thinking. Instead, fix your attention on God. You'll be changed*

from the inside out. Readily recognize what He wants from you, and quickly respond to it. Unlike the culture around you, always dragging you down to its level of immaturity, God brings the best out of you, develops well-formed maturity in you (Romans 12:1-2 MSG).

When my wife and I were first married, we were very poor, but it was OK. One weekend when she was off visiting her mother, I found a dresser for $12 at a garage sale, and we needed another dresser. The dresser's only problem was it was ugly; someone had painted it lime green. However, the paint had rubbed off one corner and I saw a little patch of walnut. I decided that underneath the ugly external coating was something worth my effort. So, I bought it, took it home, got paint remover and varnish, and started to transform it. I was very excited as I began to work on it, but after getting the ugly green paint off, I discovered an equally ugly coat of yellow paint. Then, underneath the yellow I found black paint. I became very discouraged and seriously considered giving up on it.

It was hard taking off what had been there for years, and the same can be true of us. It took me 10 or 12 hours just to remove all the layers of ugliness. However, once I got all the paint off, an unfinished, but beautiful walnut wood dresser appeared. It only took me 20 minutes to put on the varnish that made it the beautiful and functional piece of furniture I had hoped it would become. *Putting on the new was easy once the old was gone.*

The foregoing Scripture (Rom. 12:1-2) is a portrait of God working to improve our way of life. If you will hunger for God and allow His Word and His Spirit to work within you, they will transform you. They will extract from you the ugly coats of the world's culture you have collected, along with the lies you have believed about yourself, others, and God. Then, in a fraction of the time it took to strip away the "old" way of thinking, God will give you the beautiful, glistening culture of the Kingdom. At that point, you will be able to recognize the will of God, and it will begin to grow and become a greater and greater part of your life.

God Wants Your Body

That is why He says, *"...present your bodies a living sacrifice, holy, acceptable to God, which is your reasonable service"* (Romans 12:1).

Beware: The devil also wants your body. Evil spirits do not want to live in trees or haunted houses; they want to inhabit human bodies. For evil spirits to have authority on earth, they must live in and act through people. God chose to restrict His direct intervention into the affairs of humankind when He gave dominion to Adam, and then He returned it to His sons and daughters through the work of Christ on the Cross. Now God wants to send His Spirit to live in your heart to accomplish *His* will on the earth. Everyone lives under the influence of one spirit or another. What spirit are you of?

God Wants Your Mind

That is why He says, *"...be transformed by the renewing of your mind..."* (Rom. 12:2).

The Spirit of God wants to help you think accurately. Your mind is the battlefield where your future is determined. It boils down to this: You can continue to believe the lies of satan or believe God's truth about who you are, who He is, your self-worth, and the real reason you are on planet Earth.

Psychology has found that when you think differently, you act differently. That amazing discovery was the basis for a relatively new form of treatment called Cognitive Behavioral Therapy. Psychologists discovered that instead of digging up all the stuff from a person's past, they have quicker and better results by helping the person to change his or her thinking. They have finally caught up with Solomon who said about 3,000 years ago: *"For as he thinks in his heart, so is he..."* (Prov. 23:7). If you allow God to change what you believe, He can change what you do.

To really learn who you are, you have to discover who God is. Remember when Jesus asked His disciples, "Who do you think I am?" (see Matt. 16:15-20). Peter, the unsophisticated fisherman who was probably seated behind the far better-educated physician, Luke, may have waved his hand and said excitedly, "I know. I know the answer to this one." When Jesus pointed at him, he blurted out, "You are the Messiah, the Christ!" When Peter came to know who Jesus truly was, Jesus told Peter who he really was, "You are Peter, destined to be a rock in My future Church." A revelation of God changes your paradigm; it alters your life by changing your reality. Jesus said it beautifully in the Beatitudes:

> *People who don't **know God** and the way He works fuss over these things, but you know both God and how He works. **Steep your life in God-reality**, God-initiative, God-provisions. Don't worry about missing out. You'll find all your everyday human concerns will be met* (Matthew 6:32-33 MSG).

The Stronghold Perched on Your Shoulders

The enemy will try to distract you from living in your revelation of God with things of the flesh. Paul warned:

> *For though we walk in the flesh, we do not war according to the flesh. For the weapons of our warfare are not carnal but mighty in God for **pulling down strongholds, casting down arguments and every high thing that exalts itself against the knowledge of God, bringing every thought into captivity** to the obedience of Christ* (2 Corinthians 10:3-5).

Do not think the word *stronghold* in this Scripture refers to a witch coven stirring a pot of something nasty in a mountain cave while muttering curses; the stronghold is sitting on our shoulders. It is a fortress of thoughts influenced by demonic powers. However, that stronghold remains invincible only so long as the thoughts that form it remain in control. It falls apart when we replace the enemy's lies by renewing our minds with Kingdom truths. The Message Bible puts it like this:

We use our powerful God-tools for smashing warped philosophies, tearing down barriers erected against the truth of God, fitting every loose thought and emotion and impulse into the structure of life shaped by Christ (2 Corinthians 10:5).

You have the tools for dispatching the demonic lies that have limited your life. In fact, God has put *you* in charge of the continuing *re*-education of your mind. God expects us to educate ourselves in the truth and then live in the power that God's truth carries with it to accomplish its purpose. That is how Jesus could say, *"And you shall know the truth, and the truth shall make you free"* (John 8:32).

The Stronghold Over Education—Humanism

Humanism is "a system of thought that rejects religious beliefs and focuses exclusively on humans." A worldview that replaces God with man is nothing new; Eve was successfully tempted by the same thing:

*The serpent told the Woman, "You won't die. God knows that the moment you eat from that tree, you'll see what's really going on. **You'll be just like God, knowing everything**, ranging all the way from good to evil"* (Genesis 3:4 MSG).

Satan tempted Eve in three ways:

First—He tempted her to question God's good intentions toward her and Adam (His character of love) by questioning why God did not allow them to satisfy their appetites with *all* the fruit of the Garden.

Second—He then tempted her to question God's truthfulness (His righteousness) by refuting God's statement that they would die if they ate of the Tree of Knowledge of Good and Evil.

Third—He finally tempted Eve with the possibility of becoming a god herself, which would free her from the need for God. As you know, she jumped at the chance to be a god, and humankind has enthusiastically believed the lie that man is a god ever since. Today, we call that belief humanism.

The name of God is blasphemed in our greatest institutions of higher learning, creation is considered a joke, the theory of evolution is celebrated as truth, and morality and righteous living are belittled as old fashioned and outmoded. You may wonder how minds that are so bright could believe in a worldview that does not include God. However, Adam and Eve bought the lie that they did not need God, and they were far more brilliant than everyone who has lived since.

A humanistic way of believing leads to a decadent and degraded way of living. As you read the following excerpt from The Message Bible paraphrase of Romans 1:21-22 and 26-27, remember that Paul was talking about people living 2,000 years ago. See if you think things have changed.

> *…They trivialized themselves into silliness and confusion so that there was neither sense nor direction left in their lives. They pretended to know it all, but were illiterate regarding life…. Refusing to know God, they soon didn't know how to be human either—women didn't know how to be women, men didn't know how to be men. Sexually confused, they abused and defiled one another, women with women, men with men—all lust, no love…* (MSG).

If you think the world has gone crazy, you are right; however, it has always been delusional. Like Eve, many have believed satan's lie and refused to give credence to the truth. David said, *"The fool has said in his heart, 'There is no God'…"* (Ps. 14:1). And the wisest man to ever live gave us the final word on humanism: *"…Fear God. Do what He tells you. And that's it…"* (Eccles. 12:13-14 MSG). However, in a time some believe to be the "worst of times," we are on the very brink of what will be described as the "best of times"—the day of dominion, a day when the kingdoms of culture fall into the hands of believers.

The Day of Dominion

We live in the season when God is *giving* the kingdoms of culture to those who have the faith to leap into their destinies. Daniel was prophesying about our day when he announced:

*I was watching; and the same horn [power] was making war against the saints, and prevailing against them, until the Ancient of Days came, and a judgment was made in favor of the saints of the Most High, and **the time came for the saints to possess the kingdom....** Then the kingdom and dominion, and the greatness of **the kingdoms under the whole heaven, shall be given to the people, the saints of the Most High.** His kingdom is an everlasting kingdom, and all dominions shall serve and obey Him* (Daniel 7:21-22, 27).

The Spirit of Stupid

What does the "fear of God" mean? You may have heard that it means "respecting God." It certainly does mean that, but in addition, it means exactly what it says. Although God is love, a devoted Father, and many other positive things, we must never forget that He is also righteous. That means, *"God will bring every work into judgment, including every secret thing, whether good or evil"* (Eccles. 12:14). You demonstrate your *fear of God* by being "afraid to sin."

Humanism is the opposite of the fear of God. It denies His existence and pays Him no respect, and the end result is the opposite of wisdom—stupidity.

The Spirit of God is the spirit of wisdom, but the spirit of humanism is the "opposite spirit." The genius Solomon explains how anyone, even a simpleton, can get wisdom, knowledge, and understanding: *The fear of the LORD is the beginning of wisdom, and the knowledge of the Holy One is understanding* (Prov. 9:10).

Fearing God brings a reward. God richly rewarded Daniel and his three friends when they showed their fear of God by not eating foods considered unclean and by not bowing to an image of the king. Their fear of God paid off big in their positions in the mountain of government. They were considered by an ungodly king to be ten times smarter than all the greatest minds in his kingdom, and before long, he promoted them to places of great influence in the mountain of government:

> *In all matters of wisdom and understanding about which the king examined them, he found them ten times better than all the magicians and astrologers who were in all his realm* (Daniel 1:20).

Renaissance in Education

The renaissance that is upon us, I believe, will cause new Harvards, Princetons, and Yales to spring up. Either the leading institutions of higher learning in our nation will be taken back by the Kingdom of God and renewed, or God's superior system of education will cause them to be superseded and become irrelevant.

It is vitally important that believers called to the mountain of education find their places of influence in this molder of the minds and beliefs of future generations, and that parents and Christians voters use their influence to the fullest extent to bring the Kingdom of God into the mountain of education.

In the next chapter we talk about Y.O.U. You may be thinking, *I agree with what you're saying, and I want to do my part, but I don't know my purpose. I don't know where I fit into God's scheme of things.* **Where is MY mountain?** If that is where you are, I have good news: Next, we talk about how to find your future by examining your past.

CHAPTER ELEVEN

Discern, Discover, and Dominate!

It is time to discern your past, discover your purpose, and dominate the giants who stand between you and your God-intended future. God has called, created, equipped, and assigned you to a life of accomplishment, purpose, and victory. You have an assignment in the Kingdom of God. He wants you to realize your calling and find your strategic place in your mountain(s) of influence. I pray that by the end of this chapter, something will awaken deep inside you that will position you on your journey to find your reason for being. I pray you will find your passion and peace and uncover the determination to overcome any giants that stand in your path that would deter you from the course God created you for.

The Church has traditionally been good about Heaven, good about hell, but not good about earth. We can get people ready for Heaven and try to keep them out of hell, but we have little understanding about what they should do during their time on earth. However, that is changing. God saved you for a purpose; He has a mission for you that will take you into a mountain of societal influence. Before leaving earth, Jesus instructed His followers to "disciple all nations" (see Matt. 28:19), not "disciple all individuals." By this, Jesus was saying, "I want My Kingdom to be demonstrated to the nations so everyone in the world can learn how to live a life that honors God, that satisfies the deep hunger in the human heart for significance, and that fulfills his or her destiny."

Kings and Queens

You are a chosen generation, a royal priesthood, a holy nation, His own special people, that you may proclaim the praises of Him who called you out of darkness into His marvelous light (1 Peter 2:9).

- *Chosen* means that God saw you, liked you, and made you His own. You are wanted, needed, and, yes, chosen.

- *Generation* refers to a time frame; God has a destiny for you in this season.

- As *priests,* we offer sacrifices of praise with our worship and by the way we conduct our lives. However, we are more than priests.

- We are *kings*. As kings and queens, Adam's lost authority has been returned to us, and we too are called to subdue the earth and bring God's dominion to every nation and culture.

Jesus has made you royalty:

*...To Him who loved us and washed us from our sins in His own blood, and has **made us kings and priests to His God and Father, to Him be glory and dominion forever and ever. Amen*** (Revelation 1:5-6).

What Do Failures Say About Your Destiny?

The revelation of your destiny often comes from an understanding of your history. *"Jesus answered and said to them, 'Even if I bear witness of Myself,*

My witness is true, for **I know where I came from and where I am going...'"** (John 8:14). He was saying that understanding His history propelled Him into His destiny, and the same can be true for you.

Most people want to forget their histories, create new beginnings, and move on. God, however, wants to restore and reform your history and create from it a destiny. Every place the enemy has assaulted you, in that same place, you have authority through the Kingdom of God to conquer:

> *And from the days of John the Baptist until the present time,* **the kingdom of heaven has endured violent assault, and violent men seize it by force** *[as a precious prize—a share in the heavenly kingdom is sought with most ardent zeal and intense exertion]* (Matthew 11:12 AMP).

This Scripture is *not* talking about "Praise the Lord and Pass the Ammunition"—fomenting a civil revolution against the government. We *are* talking about *spiritual* violence, which means "prevailing with unyielding faith and prayer until we seize the promises of God." Operating in the Kingdom of God requires us to engage the enemy, and a violent struggle is always part of that encounter.

Have You Heard My Story?

My wife and I have a story that many people find difficult to believe. The condensed version is: We lost $20 million to a con man. We were on the front page of the local paper ten times and the subject of six lawsuits. We lost every penny we had and were homeless for a period of time. One year we even celebrated Christmas in a hotel room. We had to declare personal bankruptcy but worked hard to pay back every penny we owed. In the end, we won every lawsuit and were vindicated in the courts of any wrongdoing. But of course, that never made the paper, not even the back page.

After going through seven years of hell, I asked God, "Send me somewhere else in the world to minister. Please," I pleaded, "get me out of Phoenix." My occupation as a pastor is based on trust, and people go to a church where they trust the ministry. So I knew that I had to go elsewhere to be in ministry. However, I could not get God to see the wisdom of my line of reasoning, and when I asked Him where we should go to minister, He answered, "Phoenix." I wondered if God had read the newspaper lately, but we obediently stayed, and God has done an incredible thing. In the same city where we faced great pain and defeat, we are now experiencing victory and blessings beyond our wildest dreams.

Many of us have been trained by our culture to leave when things get tough. When our marriage becomes difficult, we leave. If our church has a problem, we go and find another. However, in the same place that hell assaulted me, God has given me an anointing greater than that assault, and He would like to do that for you.

Here Is the Key

The very thing that tried to kill you, steal from you, or destroy you, you are often assigned, anointed, and equipped by God to rule over.

Consider Moses. Born at a time when Pharaoh had ordered every male Hebrew child thrown in the river, Moses was placed in a reed boat in the crocodile-infested Nile. He was rescued by an Egyptian princess. He was raised, however, by his mother, and he lived as a prince in the house of the very man who ordered his execution. However, Moses' domestic bliss ended the day he tried to protect a fellow Hebrew and killed an Egyptian:

> *When Pharaoh heard of this matter, he sought to kill Moses* [again]. *But Moses fled from the face of Pharaoh and dwelt in the land of Midian...* (Exodus 2:15).

When Moses was 80 years old, he had an encounter with God at a burning bush. What did God tell Moses to do? Go back to the place of his defeat, meet with the man who tried to kill him, and set the ungrateful Israelites free. Moses returned to Egypt and fulfilled his destiny in the same place the enemy had assaulted him and tried to take his life.

Look at Joseph. He had dreams of reigning over his family and made the mistake of bragging a little, which caused him to be betrayed by his family, who sold him into slavery. He was purchased by a high-ranking member of the court of Pharaoh, accused falsely of rape, and finally imprisoned for a crime he did not commit. He had two great betrayals in his life: his family and the government of Egypt.

Then a day came when someone walked down the dungeon corridor to Joseph's cell, keys rattled in his lock, his cell opened, and Joseph ended up released to his destiny. (A day is coming when a key will bring you release to your destiny too!) Within a single day, Joseph went from prisoner to prime minister, from living in a prison to the comforts of the palace. The very same system that put him in prison made him the head of state. And the same family who betrayed him was saved by him. In the very place and with the very people who were responsible for the greatest attacks on his life, Joseph met his destiny:

> *Then Pharaoh took his signet ring off his hand and put it on Joseph's hand; and he clothed him in garments of fine linen and put a gold chain around his neck.... So he set him over all the land of Egypt* (Genesis 41:42-43).

Study Samson. He was a young man who had taken the Nazarene vow, the declaration to live a life of extreme holiness. However, he fell in love with a woman from the enemy's camp. You know his parents must have been upset and said, "Couldn't you find a nice Jewish girl?" The Bible says:

*But his father and mother did not know that **it was of the** LORD— that He was seeking an occasion to move against the Philistines. For at that time the Philistines had dominion over Israel (Judges 14:4).*

The Hebrew word translated *occasion* in this verse means "to start a fight." Think about it: God was angry at the Philistines who were oppressing His people. He was looking for someone to use, and of all the people available, He decided to use the guy who had made a mistake. How sad that some in the Church have created artificial categories of people whom they believe God cannot use: the divorced, those who had an abortion, people who were once addicted to drugs or alcohol, and those who made other notable mistakes. Yet, God wants to take our mistakes and failings and put them all together into a ministry that will help others.

When Samson's wife was taken from him and later killed, God used the brokenness of his heart to defeat the Philistines and bring about freedom for an entire nation. God will do the same thing with us. He wants to use our brokenness to defeat the enemy in the very area in which we were defeated and use us to bring freedom to others.

Be Thankful for Your History

Daily, I thank the Lord for everything He allowed to happen in my life because I could not be who I am today without my history. My past made me and shaped me, and now I am seeing the meaning for my history as God makes *"...All things work together for good to those who love God, to those who are the called according to His purpose"* (Rom. 8:28).

It does not matter what is in your past, how dysfunctional your family was (or is), or the kinds of heartache in your history. God wants to take the *worst things* of your history and transform them into the *best things* of your destiny.

What Are Giants Saying About You?

The pathway to your destiny will lead you through the land of giants—the giants of generational curses, personal weaknesses, discouragement, greed, pride, immorality, corruption, humanism, and fear. Each giant wants to hinder your progress or detour you from the future God has for you. When you do as David did and defeat the lion and bear and overcome your personal giants (see 1 Sam. 17:36), then you can dispatch every other giant.

Regardless of where you are today, God has a path to your destiny. Whether you are out in the pasture caring for sheep like young David or in the pigsty eating pig food like the prodigal son, there is a pathway from where you are to the place God created for you and for which you were created. However, your journey will not be a leisurely stroll through an idyllic forest; it will be far more exciting. Your pathway will take you to seemingly insurmountable mountains, ostensibly uncrossable rivers, and apparently undefeatable giants. Yet, you need not fear because Jesus traveled that way before you and overcame each of your obstacles. Your job is to merely use your faith and determination to enforce His victory:

> *Behold, I give you the authority to trample on serpents and scorpions, and over all the power of the enemy, and nothing shall by any means hurt you* (Luke 10:19).

Certain moments of your life define you, not what you say about yourself or even what others say about you. Your journey defines you, but it also prepares you. What you do—in the day of trial and tribulation, the day of adversity, the day the devil gives you his best shot and you either succumb or overcome—defines you. By giving you free will, God put the pen in your hand to write the story of your life. Regardless of the previous chapters, God will empower you to write another, better chapter and, yes, create a happy ending.

Giants Define Us

As with David, your pathway of destiny goes through battlefields with giants, and the giants you conquer will define you. However, the giants you do not conquer also define you. The entire generation of Israel that refused to enter their Promised Land was defined not by what they did but by what they would not do. Refuse to allow giants of unbelief, doubt, and fear to keep you from your rightful place. Israel's enemy and your enemy rules by fear and deception. The tactic is to make you appear small in your own eyes:

> Then Caleb…said, "Let us go up at once and take possession, for we are well able to overcome it." But the men who had gone up with him said, "We are not able to go up against the people, for they are stronger than we…. There we saw the giants…and we were like grasshoppers in our own sight, and so we were in their sight" (Numbers 13:30-31,33).

However, we do not have to accept the enemy's grasshopper point of view, and we do not attack our giants while choking back our fears, charging forward merely hoping for the best. We attack from a place of "rest," the rest that Jesus gives freely to all who become yoked with Him:

> Come to Me, all you who labor and are heavy laden, and I will give you rest. Take My yoke upon you and learn from Me, for I am gentle and lowly in heart, and you will find rest for your souls (Matthew 11:28-29).

Are you living in rest? We are intended to be peaceful warriors fighting from a place of victory rather than fighting for it. Peace and rest are our greatest weapons, "…In quietness and confidence is your strength…" (Isa. 30:15 NLT). We have to cultivate a heartfelt realization that Jesus really meant it when He said:

> Peace I leave with you, My peace I give to you…. Let not your heart be troubled, neither let it be afraid (John 14:27).

…I will never leave nor forsake you (Hebrews 13:5).

Your greater challenge is not thrashing the giant but finding your rest and retaining your peace during the battle. By doing the one, the other naturally follows. Before entering the combat zone, David did not go to the stream in panic to throw up; he went to find five smooth stones.

Are You a "Smooth Stone"?

God is looking for lives that have allowed His Word and Spirit to wash over them until they are transformed into people suitable for use in a kingdom of influence:

> *…He chose for himself five smooth stones from the brook, and put them in a shepherd's bag, in a pouch which he had, and his sling was in his hand. And he drew near to the Philistine* (1 Samuel 17:40).

Oh, and David did not take five stones because he was afraid that his first shot would miss. History tells us Goliath had four brothers.

God has chosen and appointed you for a specific mountain, and when you operate in your mountain under His authority and anointing to produce fruit, you have a blank check. He will give you "whatever you ask for":

> *You didn't choose me. I chose you. I appointed you to go and produce fruit that will last, so that the Father will give you whatever you ask for, using My name* (John 15:16 NLT).

You have an authority in *your* mountain(s) that you will not have in others. The thing that is easy for you in *your* mountain will be difficult in other mountains. Consequently, you have to find your mountain because it is there you will enter the flow of God's favor. If you are wondering why things are not flowing your way, there are three possible reasons:

1. You are in the wrong mountain.

2. It is not the right time.

3. You are not ready.

Could God be smoothing you? *"Behold, I have refined thee, but not with silver; I have chosen thee in the furnace of affliction"* (Isa. 48:10 KJV).

Where Are You Camping?

As long as the children of Israel followed the cloud by day and the fire by night whenever they moved, God protected and provided for His people. Neither they nor we can set up a permanent camp anywhere this side of the Promised Land. When they did refuse to go where God wanted to lead—the Promised Land—He took them in circles for the remainder of their lives.

Remember when Elijah announced to Elisha that he was about to relocate from earth to Heaven and asked his apprentice what he wanted as a parting gift? Elisha asked for the "double portion," and Elijah promised that he could have it *if* he was present to witness Elijah being taken up to Heaven (see 2 Kings 2). Then they set out on a journey that took them to:

- *Gilgal*—This word means "rolling" and is symbolic of the rolling away of the stone at Jesus' tomb and of salvation. Many stop and camp at salvation and miss the remainder of the trip and their double portion.

- *Bethel*—This word means "house of God" and is symbolic of the Church. You can stop and camp at becoming a member of a local church but still lose out on the fullness of your inheritance.

- *Jericho*—This word means "sweet, fragrant place" and is symbolic of the gifts and working of the Holy Spirit. You can camp, as many Pentecostals and Charismatics have, at experiencing and operating in the gifts of the Spirit, but there is even more for you.

- *Jordan*—This is the place of crossing over into the Promised Land or God's strategy for taking His Kingdom to the seven kingdoms of culture. This is the place where those who learn about the seven-mountain strategy may camp. They acknowledge its truth but never actually allow it to change their lives.

When you go all the way with God and follow Him into your mountain of destiny, you, like Elisha, can have the "double portion." But each stop along the way is important to preparing and refining you. However, do not make camp and stop following the cloud until you reach *your* promised land!

Are You Edgy?

Our lives are ultimately defined by the quality and quantity of change we allow God to bring into them. God *wants* to use everyone but He *does* not; He can only use those who have allowed themselves to be prepared. David went to the riverbed to find stones he would use to defeat the giant. On the edge of the river were stones that had never been touched by water (they symbolize those who have not found Christ as Savior). A little farther in were stones that had experienced a little water splashed on them (they symbolize "seekers" who have yet to allow themselves to be transformed). However, only those stones that had remained in the water long enough to be smoothed by the "washing of water by the Word" (see Eph. 5:26) and by the working of the Holy Spirit were prepared for His purpose.

So it is with God. He too is looking for rocks with no edges—ammunition that will be effective in the mountains of culture. A jagged stone might catch in the sling and fly off in the wrong direction and do more damage than good. An uneven rock might not be aerodynamic enough to attain the speed required to pierce its target. A rock untested by the waters might disintegrate under the pressure of battle and be destroyed. David knew something about rocks, and to be a smooth stone in the hands of God, you need to get to know David's Rock: *"He is my rock and my salvation. He is my Defender; I will not be defeated"* (Ps. 62:6 NCV).

Perhaps this gives us a new understanding of how Paul could make the outrageous statement that "we glory in tribulations" found in Romans 5:3-5:

> *We can rejoice, too, when we run into problems and trials, for we know that they are good for us—they help us learn to endure. And endurance develops strength of character in us, and character strengthens our confident expectation of salvation. And this expectation will not disappoint us. For we know how dearly God loves us, because He has given us the Holy Spirit to fill our hearts with His love* (NLT).

God brought a long-haired, harp-playing, poetry-writing, hippie-like shepherd boy out of the backwoods of total obscurity to slay the meanest and mightiest giant of his day. David went on to become the champion and finally the leader of his nation's mountain of government, and God can't wait to do the same thing for you. To take an important step on the road to your destiny, take a moment right now to ask Him to show you the defeats and losses in your history that He wants to make strengths and use to fulfill your destiny. Also, make the determination to dominate your giants. Have you looked in your spiritual mirror lately? God also sees you as a giant, a powerful, peaceful spiritual warrior. You can do this! In fact, it's what you were born and born again to do.

In the next chapter, we go prospecting for divine favor. One precious nugget of favor can raise you to a life more incredible than any you can imagine.

CHAPTER TWELVE

The Unstoppable Force of Divine Favor

Every advancement requires conflict. To take possession of that which God has given, you must wrestle it from the enemy's grasp: *"...The kingdom of heaven suffers violence, and the violent take it by force"* (Matt. 11:12). It may sound kind of scary, but the extremely good news is that you do not have to tackle satan alone in your own power and ability. God will be with you, and you will have access to the unstoppable force of divine favor. *You will not be defeated!* If you do not give up, you will win.

Out-n-In

Almost all the Church understands "out," but we have failed to grasp "in." However, redemption is a *two*-part process—out and in. We have mistakenly thought redemption was only coming out of bondage to sin, satan, and the curse of the law. We failed to understand that in addition to coming out, we are to go into the promises and power of His glorious Kingdom. The freeing of the children of Israel from the Egyptians is the Old Testament illustration of salvation. What God said to them also applies to us:

> *...I am the LORD;* **I will bring you OUT** *from under the burdens of the Egyptians, I will rescue you from their bondage, and* **I will**

redeem you with an outstretched arm and with great judgments. **I will take you as My people**, and I will be your God…. **And I will bring you INTO the land** which I swore to give to Abraham…and **I will give it to you** as a heritage: I am the LORD (Exodus 6:6-8).

There are many comparisons between the freeing of Israel from Egypt and the spiritual history of humankind, and I have listed a few that are significant to the premise of this book:

ISRAEL	HUMANKIND
When the children of Israel came to Egypt, they had favor, freedom, and a wonderful place to live.	Adam and Eve lived in paradise, the most magnificent place on earth, the Garden of Eden.
A time came when the children of Israel lost their freedom, became slaves to Pharaoh, and had to work hard to please their master and feed themselves.	Adam and Eve lost their freedom when they sinned and had to work hard to provide for themselves because the ground was cursed.
For centuries, they cried out for a deliverer. God heard them and provided Moses.	For several millennia, humankind cried for a Messiah. God heard and provided His Son.
Moses defeated Pharaoh and brought his people out of bondage through the final plague, the death of the firstborn, but the blood of an innocent lamb on the doorpost protected the Hebrews from death.	Jesus defeated sin, satan, and death by shedding His blood, and He reclaimed the keys of dominion that Adam and Eve surrendered to satan. His blood is on the doorpost of our hearts as our protection against evil.

God was Israel's Provider and Defender during their time in the desert. They were content with merely being free and had no desire to face seemingly impossible odds to step into their inheritance and destiny in the Promised Land.	God is a Christian's provider of "every good thing." The Church has been content to count its blessings rather than cross over into its promised land of inheritance in the mountains of culture.
God brought Israel *out* to take them *into* the Promised Land, but they refused to tackle their giants.	God brought Christians out of bondage to take them into their promised land of influence in society, but rather than attack the giants in the mountains of influence, we have considered them undefeatable and cursed the mountains as evil.
God waited for a generation of Hebrews who would complete the trip, take what He had given them, and plant His kingdom in the Promised Land.	God has waited for a generation of Christians (the Joshua Generation) who understand their purpose and are willing to take on the giants to possess their inheritance and assume their rightful place as Kingdom ambassadors in the mountains of culture.

God's goal was never to merely free us *from* something but to make us free *for* something.

He brought us out of sin to bring us into His Kingdom—out of satan into Christ, out of confusion into wisdom, out of sickness and pain into healing, and out of futility into supernatural purpose. God has a plan for you. He brought you out to bring you into your uniqueness, your gifts and calling, and your place of purpose and influence.

Out of the Curse and *Into* the Blessing

A short list of things that fall under the curse of the law includes: sickness, disease, mental illness, failure, poverty, anxiety, worry, fear, and a fruitless life. Because we could never keep the law as sinners, we were subject to all its curses, but:

> *Christ has* **redeemed us from the curse of the law,** *having become a curse for us (for it is written, "Cursed is everyone who hangs on a tree"),* **that the blessing of Abraham might come upon the Gentiles** *in Christ Jesus, that we might* **receive the promise of the Spirit** *through faith* (Galatians 3:13-14).

God saved us *out* of sin to put us *into* the blessing of Abraham's covenant and Kingdom significance.

Out of Darkness and *Into* the Light

> *…You are a chosen people. You are a kingdom of priests, God's holy nation, His very own possession. This is so you can show others the goodness of God, for* **He called you out of the darkness into His wonderful light** (1 Peter 2:9 NLT).

It is God's intention for you, as a warrior of His light, to demonstrate the goodness of God by merely living the supernatural life of a Christian in your mountain of influence. Through your position of cultural influence you can lead a world stumbling in the darkness, fumbling for the light switch, to the Light of the World.

Nick at Night

In the third chapter of John, Jesus explained the "new birth" to Nicodemus, a prominent leader among the Jews. You probably remember that during Nick's nighttime visit, Jesus told him, *"...unless one is born again, he cannot **see the kingdom** of God"* (John 3:3). Notice that once you are born again and come out of the world, *you can begin to see* what God is offering to humankind through His Kingdom.

A little later in their conversation, Jesus told Nicodemus, *"...Unless one is born of water and the Spirit, he cannot **enter the kingdom of God**"* (John 3:5). Jesus was explaining to Nick that once the spirit of a man is reborn and the Holy Spirit comes to live within him, he then has the spiritual perception to see the Kingdom and its purpose and to take the next step of *entering* into his Kingdom assignment.

The Lost Kingdom

God created man in His likeness (see Gen. 1:26). God- or Christlikeness is the key to our authority on the earth and over satan. The more like Jesus we are, the more authority we have. God created Adam and Eve with the ability and the tools to be the king and queen of the Garden of Eden. However, they were called to do more than preside over their Garden annex of God's Kingdom on earth. They were to enlarge its boundaries until His Kingdom filled the entire planet. *"Then, just as water covers the sea, people everywhere will know the LORD's glory"* (Hab. 2:14 NCV).

Although everything in the material world was made by God and therefore belonged to Him, God formed with Adam the Adamic Covenant, which gave the earth to humankind as a *fiefdom*, which means "a domain over which one dominant person or group exercises control." The word *covenant*, when used in the Bible, means "an agreement between God and someone in which God makes certain promises and requires certain behavior from him or her in return." Humankind's authority to rule earth is derived from the covenant God made with Adam and Eve. As the descendants of the first couple we were "in" them when the covenant was made, consequently, we are inheritors of the rights and privileges of their covenant of dominion.

Sin, however, broke humankind's covenant with God to co-partner in bringing His glory and dominion to the entire earth. That partnership ended when it became impossible for sinful man to be linked to a righteous God. By choosing to disobey God, humankind's allegiance shifted from God, the Spirit of righteousness, to satan, the spirit of unrighteousness. Consequently, the man and woman who would be king and queen lost their kingdom in the moment of their sin. The keys of power were snatched from their sin-weakened hands, and satan took over control to become the ruler of the physical realm.

However, the all-knowing God was not caught by surprise. The Trinity had created a plan for the redemption of humankind and earth even before creation, prior to Adam and Eve's "big mistake." The Trinity's secret plan was to bring the Kingdom of God back to earth and return the right of dominion to humankind so that man could regain the lost Kingdom. This was made possible by the rebirth of man into a being who could resume his connectedness with God and take up again the mission of humankind to bring the dominion of God to every corner of the earth.

Mystery Solved!

It should no longer be a mystery why Jesus was always talking about the Kingdom of God and why He said things the Church has not fully understood until recently, like:

*The time is fulfilled, and the **kingdom of God is at hand.** Repent, and believe in the gospel* (Mark 1:15).

*In this manner, therefore, pray: Our Father in heaven, hallowed be Your name. **Your kingdom come.** Your will be done on earth as it is in heaven* (Matthew 6:9-10).

Seven Kingdoms, Seven Nations, Seven Principalities

The number *seven* means "completeness or fullness." God completed creation of the physical realm and rested on the seventh day. And when the seven mountains of culture come under the influence of the Kingdom of God, the Church will have completed its work too.

The seven nations the Hebrews faced in their Promised Land are similar in many ways to, and symbolic of, the seven mountains the end-time Church is called to prevail over. The statements God made to the children of Israel in Deuteronomy 7:6 and 8 before entering the Promised Land are equally true for us:

> *You are a holy people to the* LORD *your God;*
>
> *…God has chosen you to be a people for Himself, a special treasure….*
>
> *…The* LORD *loves you…*
>
> *The* LORD *has brought you out with a mighty hand, and redeemed you from the house of bondage….*

As you move into your mountain of influence, God promises:

> *When the* LORD *your God brings you into the land which you go to possess, and has cast out many nations before you…seven nations greater and mightier than you, and **when the*** LORD ***your God delivers them over to you, you shall conquer them***… (Deuteronomy 7:1-2).

Nations—Mountains—Strongholds

Jebusites	Family	Discouragement
Amorites	Church/Religion	Pride

Canaanites	Business	Greed
Girgashites	Government	Corruption
Hivites	Education	Humanism
Perizzites	Arts/Entertainment	Immorality
Hittites	Media	Fear

It would seem obvious that the God who created the mountains of culture knows the best ways to operate in the mountains of family, church, business, government, education, arts/entertainment, and media better than any person. So, when Spirit-led people go into their mountains of influence, they can take with them God's wisdom and anointing. Consequently, they have an enormous advantage because of their anointing and wisdom, as well as the powerful force of divine favor.

Favor—Your "Piton" for Successful Mountain Climbing

Possibly the most important tool in the backpack of a mountain climber is the *piton,* which, according to *Merriam-Webster,* is "a spike, wedge, or peg that is driven into a rock or ice surface as a support for mountain climbers." Supernatural favor is the wedge that creates your place, your opening. Favor is the spike that stakes your claim, and it is the peg that provides a step to the next level.

The unstoppable force of divine favor is located in your mountain of destiny. When God delivered the Israelites from slavery to the Egyptians, He gave them their back wages:

> And **I will give this people favor** in the sight of the Egyptians; and it shall be, when you go, that you shall not go empty-handed.... So **you shall plunder the Egyptians** (Exodus 3:21-22).

We often act like we are on the losing team, as if the government mountain is too powerful; Hollywood is too wicked; the business mountain is too corrupt; the education mountain too defiant; the media mountain too frightening; and the family mountain too difficult for redemption. We would not say it, but we *act like* Christians are on the losing side in every mountain of our society. Yet, like the Hebrews when they entered their Promised Land, we have *God* on our side too.

Think about this: If God could cause Egypt to do such a crazy thing as pay the Israelites to leave Egypt, what will He do for you as you seek to take His Kingdom into the elevated places of culture?

Favor Is Found Where You Need It— in Your Mountain

Your favor is waiting for you in your mountain of destiny. When the right person (that would be you) comes to the right place (that would be your mountain assignment) at the right time (that would be God's timing), you have wild, crazy, extreme, unreasonable, extravagant *favor!*

Favor is also like a ladder positioned in your mountain. If there is no ladder of favor where you are, it means one of two things: You are in the wrong mountain or it is not yet your time. In your mountain is the *grace* to do the difficult and *favor* to do the seemingly impossible. So, find your ladder.

When You Have a Ladder, Nobody Can Hold You Down

Egypt was Joseph's promised land. His brothers thought they were ridding themselves of a nuisance when they sold him as a slave to Egypt, *but* they were just transporting Joseph to the place he was called to be.

As a slave, Joseph excelled and was put in charge of all Potiphar's affairs. (He was getting streams of favor as he neared the place of his calling.) Potiphar's wife thought that she was getting revenge when she caused Joseph to be put in prison, *but* instead she moved him closer to his calling, the mountain of government, by positioning him where he could come to the attention of Pharaoh. Even in prison, Joseph had a stream of favor when he was made the head trustee. Once the right person, Joseph, was at the right place, Egypt, at the right time, he found his ladder, and during the course of a single day, he climbed out of the dungeon to become prime minister of Egypt (see Gen. 37–41).

You've gotta find your ladder!

The ABCs of Favor

A. There is a character trait that attracts divine favor and also one that repels it. Jesus explained those two traits in Matthew 23:12:

Whoever exalts himself [with haughtiness and empty pride] shall be humbled (brought low), and whoever humbles himself [whoever has a modest opinion of himself and behaves accordingly] shall be raised to honor (AMP).

B. Pride destroys favor, so when God shows you that you have an attitude of pride; it is time to repent:

Humble yourselves in the sight of the Lord, and He will lift you up (James 4:10).

C. Favor will grow as you mature spiritually:

And Jesus increased in wisdom and stature, and in favor with God and men (Luke 2:52).

D. God has your back. As you move into your mountain and increase in favor, there will be those who come against you, but favor will protect you:

For You, O LORD, *will bless the righteous;* **with favor You will surround him** *as with a shield* (Psalm 5:12).

E. Favor has a season. If you are in your mountain and nothing seems to be happening, your day is coming:

You will arise and have mercy on Zion; for the **time to favor her**, *yes, the set time, has come* (Psalm 102:13).

F. Even ungodly people are affected by the divine favor surrounding a person:

And the LORD *had given the people favor in the sight of the Egyptians, so that they granted them what they requested. Thus they plundered the Egyptians* (Exodus 12:36).

G. The desert places of life are training in humility; they qualify us to receive favor:

And you shall remember that the LORD *your God led you all the way these forty years in the wilderness, to humble you and test you, to know what was in your heart, whether you would keep His commandments or not.... Who fed you in the wilderness with manna, which your fathers did not know, that He might humble you and that He might test you, to do you good in the end* (Deuteronomy 8:2,16).

H. David understood about favor and recognized that when you reach a place of prominence in your mountain, a time will come when you have to actively cultivate humility. You will recall that when David was crowned king, he brought the Ark of the Covenant to Jerusalem. He personally led the procession with the Ark through the city streets, all the while dancing, whirling, and spinning while stripped to his tunic. When he returned home, his wife scolded him, saying:

*"How glorious the king of Israel looked today! He exposed himself to the servant girls like any indecent person might do!" David retorted to Michal, "I was dancing before the Lord, who chose me above your father and his family! He appointed me as the leader of Israel, the people of the Lord. So I am willing to act like a fool in order to show my joy in the Lord. Yes, and **I am willing to look even more foolish than this**…"* (2 Samuel 6:20-22 NLT).

I. Favor is intended to accomplish more than merely bless you. You will be personally prospered, but God also intends that you use your favor to bless others. Esther, the orphan girl who became queen of the wealthiest and most powerful nation of her day, used favor with her husband the king to save not only herself but also her people:

*…The king again asked, "Queen Esther, what would you like? Half of my kingdom! Just ask and it's yours." Queen Esther answered, **"If I have found favor in your eyes, O King, and if it please the king, give me my life, and give my people their lives.**…** If it please the king and he regards me with favor and thinks this is right, and if he has any affection for me at all, **let an order be written that cancels the bulletins authorizing the plan of Haman…to annihilate the Jews in all the king's provinces."** …[The king replied,] "So go ahead now and write whatever you decide on behalf of the Jews; then seal it with the signet ring"…* (Esther 7:2-3; 8:5,8 MSG).

The Most Important Thing to Remember About Favor

When God's favor makes you a king or queen in your mountain of influence, remember: It was God who put you there. You are in charge of maintaining your humility, and you are called to use your favor as a force for the Kingdom of God. Also, never forget that you reign in your mountain of influence because of the gift of "one man":

> *One man sinned, and so death ruled all people because of that one man. But now those people who accept God's full grace and the great gift of being made right with Him* **will surely have true life and rule through the one man, Jesus Christ** (Romans 5:17 NCV).

In the final chapter, we talk about your strategy for becoming king (or queen) of your mountain. We will seek out little-known truths about divine positioning, purpose, and provision. Are you ready to grab the tow bar to the top of your slope?

CHAPTER THIRTEEN

Divine Positioning, Purpose, and Provision—The Launching Pad to Your Destiny

In this final chapter, I want to focus on where you are today, how you got there, what God is up to in your life, and how He will get you from where you are to the position for which you were created. Many Christians think they should be further along their paths to spiritual maturity, and after reading the preceding chapters, you may wonder if you are even further behind than you thought. However, I beg to differ. Today, you are exactly where you are supposed to be—and I think I can prove it to you.

Our Western way of thinking would have us believe that we are the masters of our fate, the authors of our destiny. Although this is true on a certain level, it is not the entire story. Some might argue that poor decisions, bad luck, disasters, or misfortunes have influenced the course of their lives, and although that, too, may be true, it is not the whole truth either. This way of looking at your life leaves out one very important factor: the *sovereignty* of God. This spiritual truth tells you that in spite of what the enemy has done to you or what you have done to yourself, God has been at work, often behind the scenes, to bring you to where you are today.

Regardless what you may believe to be true about your present circumstances, you are actually located at a crossroads today, positioned at a jumping-off point, and perfectly poised for a new beginning. In fact, I believe it is no coincidence that you are holding this book at this moment in time or that God has brought this teaching to you during this season of your life. This is your opportunity to fulfill your reason for existence by entering into your God-given destiny.

The Unsinkable Man

If you are not sure that you can buy into the *sovereignty* of God affecting your life, then consider the story of Joseph as we look at it from a different point of view:

> *And Joseph said to his brothers, "Please come near to me." So they came near. Then he said: "I am Joseph your brother, whom you sold into Egypt. But now, do not therefore be grieved or angry with yourselves because* **you sold me here***; for* **God sent me** *before you to preserve life. ... To preserve a posterity for you in the earth, and to save your lives by a great deliverance. So now* **it was not you who sent me here, but God***...* (Genesis 45:4-8).

Two Important Lessons from Joseph

- Joseph told his brothers not to "grieve" over what they had done. Grief can be a blindfold that hides the truth. You cannot see the purpose of God *today* if grief has you focused on *yesterday*.

- Joseph had to get past the method God used to get him to Egypt before he could enter into his purpose. We too cannot afford to get hung up on the ways God uses to move us from one place to another or we could miss out on the incredible things He has for us there.

Can you look at your past messes and see that God used them to get you where you are today? Can you see the fingerprints of God on your life as Joseph could? Do you really believe, as Paul did, *"…That **all things** work together for **good** to those who **love** God, to those who are the **called** according to His **purpose**"* (Rom. 8:28)?

You can apply this well-known Scripture to your life by answering a few questions:

1. Do you *love* God?

2. Are you *called* to a mountain of influence? (Everyone is.)

3. Does God have a *purpose* for your life? (Everyone does.)

4. Then is God working in your stuff, your *"all things,"* to make them turn out for your good?

5. What does God consider to be your *good?* Your definition and His might differ (His may not include a new BMW). However, God's definition of *good* is not only much better than yours, but it also positions you to better pursue your purpose and fulfill your destiny.

When sailing to Rome to appeal his case to Caesar, Paul advised the ship's captain and his centurion escort to wait until the stormy season was over before continuing their journey. He was not speaking prophetically but practically. However, being in a hurry, they set sail anyway. Just as Paul had predicted, they were soon in the deadly winds of a typhoon. The weather was so bad that they did not see the sun or stars for weeks, and even the ship's seasoned sailors gave up all hope of making it to safety. When hope was gone, Paul got a word from God that they would all be saved but the ship and cargo would be lost. Just as no storm could take Jesus' life, a storm could not take Paul's life either; he was unsinkable like Jesus because he had a God-given destiny to go to Rome. The angel said to Paul:

Do not be afraid, Paul; you must stand before Caesar; and behold, God has granted you all those who are sailing with you (Acts 27:24 NASB).

One person of destiny can save an airplane that would otherwise crash. One person of purpose can change a nation. Your purpose and destiny can make you unsinkable too!

Turbulence Means Change

Everyone wants to have a dynamic purpose for his or her life, but few want to make the journey that a heroic purpose requires. In chapter 1 of the Book of Ruth, we find the story of three women and three men, but by the end of the chapter, the story contains only the three female characters. Naomi and her husband, Elimelech, left Bethlehem during a famine and moved to Moab with their two sons. While there, the sons took wives, but after a time the father died and his two sons soon followed him to the grave. Consequently, a broken-hearted Naomi and her grieving daughter-in-law Ruth return home to Bethlehem. (The other widow returned to her family.) Naomi was bitter about this change in her life and renamed herself *Mara*, meaning "bitter," claiming that God had dealt with her bitterly.

Sometimes when we taste change, all we sense is the bitterness of the events that compelled us into the change. However, Naomi and Ruth's purpose could not be fulfilled in Moab, and sometimes God uses tragedy, grief, failure, or even death to move us to the place we need to be to connect with our destinies. But if we focus on the *method* God used to get us where we are, we can fail to recognize His *message* for repositioning us and miss our blessing. We will be unable to hear what God is saying if we allow bitterness or negative emotions to shout louder than God's message.

"Why" Is the Wrong Question

To ask God "why" a thing happens is always the wrong question because it is a *victim* question. God never sees us as victims, and He refuses to speak to the spirit of fear. The right questions to ask Him in unusual times are those found in the second chapter of Acts.

The people who witnessed the initial outpouring of the Holy Spirit asked:

1. What does it mean?

2. What should I do?

These questions free us to enter into our present purpose rather than make us slaves to past events.

You may recall that Naomi and Ruth had nothing when they arrived in Bethlehem, and Ruth went to glean in the harvest fields behind the reapers to get them food to eat. God had instructed the Israelites to always leave something behind in the fields for the needy; this was His way of providing for the poor. The Bible says, *"...And **she happened** to come to the part of the field belonging to Boaz, who was of the family of Elimelech"* (Ruth 2:3).

Boaz was a kinsman of Elimelech, Naomi's deceased husband. Even in the midst of tragedy, God will make things just "happen." God is still in charge of your life even when you are grieving over a loss. When you need Him the most, you are going to happen onto a miracle provision. Within a few verses, Ruth "happens" to go from a destitute widow to the wife of the richest, most eligible bachelor in Bethlehem.

God is positioning you to run into your Boaz, to come across *your* miracle. Psalm 37:23 says, *"The steps of a good man* [or woman] *are ordered by the LORD, and He delights in his way."* In your moments of despair, you are not alone. Fate is not directing your course. God is in control—yes, even in the worst of times.

Your job in times of trouble is to, *"**Trust in the Lord and do good**. Then you will live safely in the land and prosper"* (Ps. 37:3 NLT). When you cannot understand God, trust Him nevertheless. Instead of feverishly trying to figure out what God is doing, simply, calmly, *"**Trust in the** LORD *with all your heart*, **and lean not on your own understanding**"* (Prov. 3:5).

Don't Allow Process to Steal Your Purpose

The reason you are where you are right now is because God has an important assignment, a Kingdom purpose, for you at that location. (Wherever you are located while reading this sentence, God needs you there. At some point He may move you, but He needs you where you are right now!)

As Joseph lay on his death bed, he said to his brothers concerning their selling him into slavery, *"...You meant evil against me, but God meant it for good in order to bring about this present result, to preserve many people alive"* (Gen. 50:20 NASB). The Hebrew word translated *meant* used twice in this Scripture comes from the word for *weaving.* Joseph was saying that although his brothers had tried to weave evil against him, God took up the weaver's beam and rewove circumstances for the good. It was not only for Joseph's good, although he had become a very wealthy and powerful man, but also for the good of his family, the nation of Egypt, and the entire Middle East. This is what God does in our situations, problems, tragedies, mistakes, failures, and losses: He becomes involved in them to reweave things so they will turn out for our good and the good of all.

What if Ruth had been bitter like Naomi and in her mourning rejected Boaz? Instead of making known to him her availability, what if she had told him, "I've had one man in my life who let me down. I don't need another"? She could have missed out on her purpose and place in the genealogy of Jesus, and Naomi would have lost the joy of raising her grandchildren. In the midst of your tempest, instead of becoming bitter and angry at God or others or becoming discouraged and defeated, be alert for things that seemingly just happen. Your Boaz, your miracle, could be waiting for you in the harvest field. Don't miss your purpose because you cannot get over the process.

Shower, Shave, Suit Up, and Smell Your Best

You have to look your best when you feel your worst:

> *Then Naomi her mother-in-law said to her, "My daughter, shall I not seek security for you, that it may be well with you? Now Boaz, whose young women you were with, is he not our relative? In fact, he is winnowing barley tonight at the threshing floor. Therefore* **wash** *yourself and* **anoint** *yourself,* **put on your best garment** *and go down to the threshing floor…"* (Ruth 3:1-3).

When things are at their worst and you are living in the midst of defeat, setbacks, loss, trauma, or injury, you have to be the best you have ever been. You cannot dress for disaster but for success. Nor can you let your negative feelings come out of your mouth. You cannot afford to fall into the trap of using self-pity as a device to get positive attention and become an emotional beggar hoping someone will pity you enough to be your savior. You already have a Savior, but He does not pity you; He loves you and has a provision for this moment of your life. So, change clothes and send your suit of sackcloth and ashes to the cleaners. If you wear the grief of yesterday, you will miss the purpose of today.

When you, like the three Hebrew children, end up walking though the fire, it will have no power over you (unless you give it power), and you will come through without even the smell of smoke. Isaiah explained it like this:

> *…Don't be afraid, I've redeemed you. I've called your name. You're mine. When you're in over your head, I'll be there with you. When you're in rough waters, you will not go down. When you're between a rock and a hard place, it won't be a dead end—because I am God, your personal God…* (Isaiah 43:1-3 MSG).

Find Your Purpose at His Feet

God will unlock your purpose when you lay at His feet. Naomi told Ruth:

> *Then it shall be, when he [Boaz] lies down, that you shall notice the place where he lies; and you shall go in, uncover his feet, and **lie down; and he will tell you what you should do*** (Ruth 3:4).

Ruth was not inviting Boaz to have sex when she uncovered his feet and lay down by them. Uncovering his feet was a reminder to Boaz of his right and divine obligation to be a kinsman redeemer to Ruth. By lying down, she was showing her consent to be redeemed by him. Boaz, the kinsman redeemer, is a powerful symbol of Christ, the Kinsman Redeemer for all humankind. Should you resist going to God and laying your life, your purpose, your grief, your very reason to live at His feet, you can miss hearing Him tell you what *you* should do.

Back to the Beach

Let's go back and find shipwrecked Paul as he staggers out of the frigid water onto the sandy beach of the island of Malta. *Malta* means "flowing with honey." Are you ready to go to your "land of milk and honey," a euphemism for the Promised Land? But what if you got to your promised land by shipwreck? Would you consider it ill-fated or fortunate, a depressing finish or a difficult beginning to something good?

When Paul and his companions made it to shore and finally got out of the chilly waters, it was raining and cold. No doubt the wind was blowing and they were miserable. However, Paul's journal says, *"The natives showed us unusual kindness; for they kindled a fire and made us all welcome…because of the cold"* (Acts 28:2). Paul did not remain at the bonfire; he jumped up and started serving and working toward their survival. *"When Paul had gathered a bundle of sticks and laid them on the fire, a viper came out because of the heat, and fastened on his hand"* (Acts 28:3). Paul was having a bad day. In the morning, he was shipwrecked and in the evening bitten by a snake.

When you try to stir up any kind of spiritual fire, demonic spirits will come out of it and try to attack you. However, Paul knew that Jesus had promised, *"They will pick up serpents, and if they drink any deadly poison, it will not hurt them…"* (Mark 16:18 NASB). So he merely shook the snake off into the fire. When God puts you on a stage where people will notice circumstances that are hurtful to you, He has a purpose in it. It is always a setup when God allows an audience to watch your *downfall* because there will come a time of *rising up* that will reveal His grace and bring a testimony to your life. To reach that desired end, you will have to overcome your mind and reasoning and merely trust God.

When Paul's audience to the snake attack *"had waited a long time and had seen nothing unusual happen to him,* **they changed their minds** *and began to say that he was a god"* (Acts 28:6 NASB). The episode with the snake was God's way of giving Paul instant influence on Malta. Soon, the leading man of the island, Publius, welcomed them into his home. Publius' father was sick, so Paul prayed and healed the man, and then every sick person on the island came to Paul to receive healing.

By the time Paul left the island, three months later, Malta had lived up to its name and become a place where the honey flowed for Paul. Instead of living on the cold, rainy beach in a straw hut, Paul lived in the mansion of Publius. Knowing Paul, we can be certain that as he held his healing crusade, he also introduced them to the Good News, and many must have been born again. How do you think Paul felt about his shipwreck the morning he boarded a ship bound for Rome—good experience or bad one?

However, what would those three months on Malta have been like had Paul "copped an attitude" and become angry at God? What if Paul had refused to let go of his questions about why God allowed a shipwreck in his life? What if Paul had refused to forgive those whose poor judgment caused the problem? What if, after being saved from death at sea, Paul had drowned himself in self-pity? The answer is: Paul's results on Malta would have been the same as ours when we allow the storms of life to blow away our faith in the goodness of God.

Kidnapped—An Opportunity of Purpose

You may remember the story of Naaman, the renowned Syrian army general, who was also a leper. (The story is found in Second Kings 5.) A young Hebrew girl, probably a teenager, was kidnapped during a raid and ended up a servant to Mrs. Naaman. Although she was living with and serving the very people who had kidnapped her, ruined her life, and stolen her future, she decided not to waste an opportunity of purpose. Instead of despising her captor, she told him how to be healed.

She mentioned the prophet in Samaria, Elijah, who had the power to heal. Naaman went to Israel and eventually received his miracle by dipping himself in the muddy Jordan River. Her witness of the power and the goodness of God to this man was also a witness to his nation. And it was made possible by a slave-girl's obedience in the midst of personal loss and trauma. Can you obey God when you are at a place you don't want to be? Should you find someone in your place of despair who needs to hear the Good News, would you be able to overcome your grief and loss to share it?

Secrets of Divine Provision and Authority

You should probably memorize the following statement, highlight it, circle it, write it in your Bible, and make a point of remembering it to your dying day. However, do not forget that you have to meet all the requirements to be issued this blank check:

When you are in the right place at the right time, in that moment you have the authority to ask for anything you need to accomplish God's purpose for your life.

After the conquest of Israel by Persia, Nehemiah was a Hebrew captive who had risen as high as a slave could go. He was the cupbearer for King Artaxerxes (see Neh. 2:1). When Nehemiah heard about the broken and burned condition of the gates and walls of Jerusalem, his passion was awakened and he found his purpose. (Remember: Your passion will always drive your purpose.) The next day when he went to work, Nehemiah could not keep the grief off his countenance even though showing a sad face to the king was punishable by death.

Instead of ending Nehemiah's life, the king asked him what was wrong and then what Nehemiah would need to make things right. When the king saw Nehemiah's passion and purpose, he, in effect, gave Nehemiah his credit card and said, "Git-R-Done." Nehemiah, the slave who had nothing but a God-given desire to rebuild the walls and gates of his hometown, received from the king letters that provided him safe passage, the materials required, and the manpower needed to rebuild Jerusalem. Nehemiah had such favor with Artaxerxes that he also had armed bodyguards to ensure his safety.

We have it backward: We have asked for divine provision before discovering God's divine purpose. Instead of wrestling spiritually for God's provision for our personal needs, we need to connect with God's purpose and gain access to resources beyond our wildest imaginations. Like Ruth, we will find our provision when we get in the right field.

When Ruth was gleaning in the field of Boaz, he instructed his harvesters: *Let fall also some of the **handfuls of purpose** for her, and leave them, that she may glean them, and rebuke her not"* (Ruth 2:16 KJV). As Ruth followed the harvester down the rows, she found "handfuls of purpose"—bundles of grain or provisions—that had been placed in her path. Someone has already walked through your tomorrow and laid down provisions for you too. All you have to do is pick up what you need. You may be thinking, *Well, that isn't happening for me!* And you may be right; however, when you are in your field (your designated mountain of influence) and know your purpose, you *will* discover your provisions waiting for you.

Turn the Tables on the Enemy

Queen Esther, after defeating the anti-Semite Haman, found that her job was not yet over. (Haman's defeat is a picture of satan's defeat by Christ on the Cross.) Although Haman had been defeated, his works lived on: The letters he had sent to the provinces where the Hebrews lived ordering their annihilation were still valid and operative. And so it is with the devil. Christ defeated satan, and he could be no more defeated than he is at this moment. However, the fight is not over because satan's works continue on the earth in every mountain of societal influence. However, God has a plan to take back those mountains, and He is empowering us, just as the king did Esther, to fight and overcome the works of satan.

Esther came once again into the presence of the king and begged to have Haman's orders revoked. You know that you are in your purpose when God opens His checkbook. He opens it widest when your need is not about you but about your purpose and the people you are called to help through your position. King Ahasuerus replied, to all intents and purposes, "I'll sign anything you write, my darling":

> *You yourselves write a decree concerning the Jews, as you please, in the king's name, and seal it with the king's signet ring; for whatever is written in the king's name and sealed with the king's signet ring no one can revoke* (Esther 8:8).

That may remind you of something Jesus once said: *"...If you ask the Father for anything in My name, He will give it to you"* (John 16:23 NASB).

Why, you may wonder, have we not seen those kinds of miraculous results? It is because we have not positioned ourselves in our mountains of influence and have not understood the divine purpose of God for ourselves and for this season of time. However, when we find our passions, capture our purpose, and seize our positions, we get God's permission to have everything we need:

> *On the thirteenth day of the twelfth month, the month of Adar, the king's order came into effect. This was the very day that the enemies of the Jews had planned to overpower them, but **the tables were now turned**: the Jews overpowered those who hated them!* (Esther 9:1 MSG)

You are located exactly where you are supposed to be right now, and God is ready to turn the tables for your benefit. Do not despise the method of transportation God used to get you here. Do not live under the influence of anger and other negative emotions against those who hurt you during your journey to this moment—those who abandoned you, broke you, or stole from you. God has something very important for you to do for His Kingdom in your mountain of influence right here…right now.

I Want to Pray for You

Lord, I ask that You awaken Your purpose and Your plan inside of each person reading these words. Thank You for leading us to a season when we will move into a realm of miraculous results. We know that we did nothing to deserve this turnaround but that it is the result of accepting Your plan and will for our lives. Help us to become clearer in our understanding of our Kingdom assignment. We release pain, anger, and unforgiveness against those who have brought us to this point. I ask You to heal those who have been wounded, traumatized, and afflicted because of the violence of their journeys to this moment. You healed me; heal them in Jesus' name! We lay ourselves at Your feet; tell us what we should do. Amen.

In this book, I've shared what God has been saying to me about the end-time season we are in. If we were standing face to face, I would look you in the eyes and ask, "What will you do with what you now know? Will you just nod, give mental assent, and go on with life as usual, or will you begin the adventure for which God created you?" Then I would challenge you with these words: "Dare to believe, and ask God to shine His light on the next step toward your place in your mountain of influence."

You have always known that you were on earth for a reason and have probably wondered if what you have now is all there is to life. But now you know how to *Turn the World Upside Down*, and you recognize that God has placed a calling upon your life to ascend to a place of satisfaction, significance, prosperity, purpose, and yes, influence, in a mountain of culture. Speaking as a prophet of the Lord, I want to announce: *"This is your moment. Enter into your destiny!"*

About Michael Maiden

Dr. Michael Maiden is the senior pastor of Church For The Nations in Phoenix, Arizona along with Pastor Mary, his beloved wife of 30 years. He strongly and lovingly prepares God's people for service in God's Kingdom. The messages are always relevant, timely, and life-changing as well as prophetic.

Dr. Maiden has earned both a Master's and Doctorate degree in Christian Psychology. He has authored seven books including The Joshua Generation: God's Manifesto for the End Time Church. In addition to his work in the local church, he is a strong prophetic voice to his generation and has ministered to those holding public office as well as pastors and ministers throughout the world. He serves on the apostolic board of Church On The Rock International—a dynamic ministry that oversees 6,000 plus churches worldwide. He is also on the board of Fishers of Men International, the Jewish Voice International and several local churches.

www.cftn.com